The New American Medicine Show

Other Books by the Author
MAGIC, MYSTICISM AND MODERN MEDICINE
TIME, SPACE AND THE MIND
THE HEALING MIND

The New American Medicine Show

Discovering the
Healing Connection

by Dr. Irving Oyle

UNITY PRESS SANTA CRUZ

PUBLISHED BY UNITY PRESS
113 NEW STREET, SANTA CRUZ, CA 95060

Christina's World (1948) by Andrew Wyeth, Page 75
Tempera on gesso panel, $32\frac{1}{4}'' \times 47\frac{3}{4}''$
Collection, The Museum of Art, New York

Oyle, Irving, 1925 –
  The new american medicine show
  Bibliography: p.
    1. Medicine, Psychosomatic.   2. Mind and body.
  3. Mental healing.   I. Title.
  RC49.O94   616.08   78-31345

COVER DESIGN: BILL PROCHNOW & DOUG RUSSO
BOOK DESIGN: CRAIG CAUGHLAN
TYPOGRAPHY: OLD STYLE #7 BY JONATHAN PECK

PRINTED IN THE UNITED STATES OF AMERICA

2 3 4 5 6 7 8 9

Contents

Acknowledgements

The author and publisher gratefully acknowledge the contribution of the following individuals whose work was so important in this book's coming to fruition.

Fritjof Capra, Ph.D.
Meyer Friedman, M.D.
Jerry Green
Thomas H. Holmes, M.D.
Peter Koestenbaum, Ph.D.
Elisabeth Kübler-Ross, M.D.
Max Parrott, M.D.
Karl Pribram, M.D.
Hans Selye, M.D.
C. Norman Shealy, M.D., Ph.D.
William A. Tiller, M.D.

Special acknowledgement to the people at the Extension Division, University of California at Santa Cruz, where creative activity made possible the following seminars upon which much of the material is based:

On the Nature of Reality
The Nature and Management of Stress
Birth and Re-Birth

Having been convinced
there was only ONE way —
the way of logic, rationality, science
the left-cerebral hemisphere
the way of the West

We discovered another —
the forgotten language of the dream
of intuition
wholeness
art
the right-cerebral hemisphere
the way of the East

Now we move to synthesize the two:

East and West
art and science
left and right

and in that process
we discover
worlds unknown
realities unseen

— DARLA CHADIMA

Foreword

DR. OYLE has written another fascinating book and done it in his own enthusiastic manner which may help more individuals recognize that the true determinants of health are those that are virtually totally under our own control. As has been pointed out by numerous individuals, most of us are born healthy and become ill largely through a poor lifestyle or poor habit. Dr. Oyle has particularly stimulated thinking in relation to the "psychosomatic aspects of health and disease." There is a rising consciousness among physicians, other health professionals and the public at large of the effect of emotions upon our health.

We should recognize, of course, that emotions are only one of the three major determinants of health. Nutrition is perhaps the most basic of all, for nutrition is increasingly inadequate in this country, with seventy-five percent of the caloric intake being deficient in vitamins and minerals and of poor quality. Without the proper nutritional building blocks, the mind cannot function adequately and undoubtedly this contributes to a significant portion of the emotional distress that does exist.

Physical exercise is also one of the great balances of the functions of the body and the mind. As Americans become increasingly less active we can expect increasing of problems both physically and mentally; but it does require proper thinking, the adequate use of intelligence, and control of emotions and habits to achieve health. This was probably understood in the days of Paracelsus. During this century, especially in the last thirty years, there has been increasing reliance upon drugs and surgery and a tendency by many people in medicine to ignore the crucial role of the psyche.

Dr. Oyle is one of the new breed of physicians who are returning to the fundamental principles of good psychosomatic medicine. As a medical student I was taught that eighty-five percent of all the problems that I would ever see would be psychosomatic in nature. Dr. Franz Ingelfinger, editor of the *New England Journal of Medicine,* two years ago emphasized that eighty percent of modern illnesses are "either self-limited or not treatable by modern medicine or surgery." Dr. Eugene A. Stead, Jr., professor of medicine at Duke University and editor of *Circulation,* has emphasized that only fifteen percent of modern medicine is scientific.

From a wide variety of prominent physicians we are increasingly made aware that patients must assume responsibility for their own health. The major determinants of health — nutrition, physical exercise, and mental attitude — are not treatable by someone else but must be self-determined. Dr. John Knowles, president of the Rockefeller Foundation, has emphasized that the "next great advance in health of the American people will come not from laboratories or hospitals, but from what people learn to do for themselves." One of the major things that people can do for themselves is use their minds to practice good relaxation and visualization techniques such as those emphasized in Dr. Oyle's book. Dr. Carl Simonton and his wife Stephanie have used such techniques in enhancing the treatment of cancer patients. At the Pain and Health Rehabilitation Center we have found relaxation and visualization techniques to be the single most important therapy which we can offer to chronically ill individuals with a wide variety of problems ranging from high blood pressure through rheumatoid arthritis to cancer and chronic debilitating pain.

Dr. Thomas McKeown, one of England's most prominent physicians, has emphasized that the role of medicine today is to teach people the principles of self-responsibility and good habits. Dr. Jerome Frank, professor of psychiatry at Johns Hopkins, and Dr. Irvine Page of the Cleveland Clinic have emphasized the importance of faith in the healing process. Books like Dr. Oyle's help individuals to understand and help to enhance faith. As you read through this book, think and experience, and as you do so you should reap the benefit of improved health.

C. NORMAN SHEALY, M.D., 1978
La Crosse, Wisconsin

Introduction

WELCOME to the magic theatre. The price of admission: an *open mind*. Hermann Hesse's hero, Steppenwolf, paid the price and passed through the portals into another world. You, dear reader, are invited to do the same. What do I mean when I say *mind*? Let's arbitrarily define *mind* as that select circle of theories, ideas, and notions about the world which we believe to be true; our storehouse of *facts*.

'To make up one's mind' regarding a statement or an assumption is to firmly accept it as truth or to reject it as falsehood. 'To go out of one's mind' is to radically alter our view of that which we call *reality*.

Well, now we have to define *reality*, don't we? Once again language gives us a hint. If you 'lose your reason' or 'take leave of your senses', you are considered to be 'out of touch with reality', and a good candidate for incarceration, tranquilization, or some combination of the two. *Reality*, the real world, is supposed by many to consist of hard, solid matter — things. Things that really matter are said to be experienced through the five senses. Thus we hear sensible people saying, "If I can touch it, I know it's real." "Seeing is believing," others agree. Reality, then, is equated with the realm of the senses.

Yet we hear perfectly reasonable people saying, "I couldn't believe my eyes!" That statement represents a leap across a chasm — a quantum jump in consciousness. It pictures a state of mind in which we realize that our senses can betray us and fool us. What's more convincing than the evidence of our own touch, hearing, and vision? Reason. Why? Because we decide that it is. Reality, according to our currently conventional belief structure, consists of the realm of the senses as experienced through a lens or a filter. The lens, installed in the course of our education and acculturation processes, impels us to focus our experience of the world, to make it conform to the basic beliefs, opinions, and 'shoulds' of our particular culture. We tend to filter out and ignore sensory information which seems unreasonable and unscientific. But the basic beliefs, opinions, and 'scientific facts' of our society are changing with mind-boggling speed — and so is our reality.

You may not be aware of this, but science hasn't explained everything. Mathematics, the most exact of our sciences, has its mysteries, inconsistencies, and paradoxes. In this age of electronic miracles, scientists still do not understand electricity. In physics, we are now probing phenomena which take place beyond the range of our equipment. Quarks, it seems, leave no tracks in bubble chambers. Contrary to popular belief, unanswered questions relative to basic phenomena abound in the science of applied biology, mother of the physician's art — questions like: What is life? Is a virus a living creature or merely a chemical compound? What event identifies the instant of death? Precisely when does a fertilized ovum become a human being? Why do some patients with terminal cancer show spontaneous remissions and inexplicably recover while others relentlessly wither and die?

Reaching the point where nature refuses to divulge her secret, the scientist turns to philosophy. He or she dreams up an operating hypothesis, a theoretical 'explanation', and proceeds as if the theory were the fact. If one is not alert, the theory, the 'as if', hardens into a belief. This belief may be later disproved, yet it continues to color the believer's perceptions, experiences, and actions. Once we've constructed an attractive operating hypothesis, we are reluctant to give it up; we tend to get nasty and aggressive when its validity is questioned. Consider, for example, the reaction of church officials to Galileo's insistence that the Earth is not the center of the solar system.

Our fundamental ideas about who we are and how we stay healthy are changing under the impact of new data. We used to think that the physical body in time-space was the only thing that mattered. We now have experimental evidence which suggests that emotions, thoughts, and beliefs matter as well. As we proceed, we will be examining some new hypotheses, contemplating different models of life and reality to see which can help maintain a state of health and well-being as we pass through this plane of existence.

For three hundred years, scientists have been scrupulously scrutinizing the world outside the human skull. In addition to tools like the telescope, cloud chamber, microscope, and oscilloscope, they have used a process called *the scientific method*. What is the purpose of all this scrutinizing, classifying, and cataloguing? Survival! Those three-dimensional, solid, real things out there — things that we see, hear, touch, taste, and smell — can harm us. They can even kill. It is this destructive propensity that leads us to dissect and dismember Mother Nature. We feel the need to understand her in order to protect ourselves against her periodic rampages. Having set out to conquer nature, the human mind created the miracle of modern technology. How has the battle gone? Nature remains unvanquished at this writing, while humanity is an endangered species. Where did we go wrong?

We have, by and large, accepted the cosmology hypothesized by the rational scientific mind. We have accepted the theorizings of science and scientists as an adjunct to, if not a substitute for, religious gospel. All major religions regard creation as a unity. Many scientists, using the analytic method, splinter that unity into pieces and study each piece by breaking it up into still smaller pieces until the fragments, subatomic particles, become so small that they disappear from our plane of existence. Studying parts — organs, atoms, electrons, quarks, and the like — tends to breed specialized thinking, which, absorbed in its own particular cul-de-sac, fails to see the forest for the trees, or the patient for the disease. Catalogued and cubbyholed in the modern medical mind are diseases, organs, tissues, cells, and chemical compounds. Like curious teenagers, we have dismantled the human body, but we can't always get it back together so it works like it's supposed to. In the words of the poet John Donne, " . . . 'tis all in pieces, all coherence gone."

The most fundamental task of our time may be to restore that coherence, to show, as Buckminster Fuller has suggested, that the whole is greater than the sum of its parts. The role of physicians in this task is, quite simply, to restore the healing connection. That is, the connection between the patient who says "I'm sick," the malfunctioning physical body which he or she brings in for repair, and the environment in which they usually function. The healing connection lies in the most elusive part of the patient, the part which 'inhabits' the body and 'lives' in the environment. The psyche, the human function usually associated with the *mind*, gives coherence and purpose to the functioning of our isolated, individual organs. If the whole is greater than the sum of its parts, my psyche, the part that says 'I', 'me', and 'mine', must be more than the simple sum of these mechanical marvels which keep me alive and conscious — my body and its organs.

The *Healing Connection* refers to the connection between ourselves and our experience — our bodies, our minds, and our environment. Those connections are being healed in society at large, and in reuniting they produce healing: a return to a state of health or wholeness. This kind of healing (the reconnection between ourselves and our experience, the observer and that which is observed) is progressing rapidly in our society. The rate is currently reflected in terms of the swift rise in public acceptance of concepts like *psychosomatic medicine, ecology,* and *holistic health.*

How can one experience this kind of healing on a personal level? One can reestablish the connection between one's self and one's experience by removing the lenses or mind-sets through which we usually see things. These lenses consist of preconceived notions about how things are, or worse, how they *should* be. It's like being nearsighted. With my glasses off, I see the world as it is; I see it with my own eyes. Fuzzy, unfocused, and full of beautiful, everchanging colored shapes streaming together like some enormous three-dimensional kaleidoscope, a magical theater. I look through my glasses, and I see the world as I've been told it should be — hard-edged; made up of discrete entities with sharp, impenetrable borders.

Which is the real world? Philosopher Immanuel Kant says that what's really out there, the 'thing in itself' (*Ding an sich*), body and environment, is unknowable. Adopting the pragmatic position of fellow physician William James, I might say, "Who cares? Choose the lens which makes you feel good, avoid the one that makes you sick." If you find that you are getting sick a lot or experiencing an undue amount of suffering, consider the possibility that your lenses, your current mind-sets about reality and 'being realistic', need changing. If you're constantly bumping into life and getting more than your fair share of bumps, bruises, and physical illnesses, maybe your lenses, your belief structures, need changing. Lenses which purport to improve one's natural view of one's own reality must be reexamined frequently and changed when necessary. Otherwise they tend to get rigid, stale, and pathogenic, distorting the reality they are supposed to clarify. This distortion renders the unfortunate wearer (or believer) prone to physical symptoms, accidents, and a general sense that life isn't working.

A common component of the syndrome of outworn lenses is frustration and irritability. This is because the person experiencing the world through them is unaware that the problem lies in the lenses. He or she believes the world is at fault. The problem lies in the belief. Understanding and accepting the connection between the symptoms and the lenses, the suffering and the belief, we remove the distorting lens and healing happens.

You are invited to set aside your beliefs about how things really are and look at the world as it appears through the eyes of modern scientists, philosophers, and physicians, men and women whose work foreshadows the dawning of the twenty-first century. Examine the world through their eyes, and see if it improves your life experience. Your own lenses are always available to you. Try the new ones. Compare them with your own and choose the ones which make you feel best. Avoid the ones which make you sick.

PART I

Stalking Health

"Specialization: Getting to know more and more about less and less until we know everything about nothing."

— ANONYMOUS

1/The Human Factor

*"Common to all . . . 'human' mechanisms — and
without which they are imbecile contraptions —
is their guidance by a phantom captain."*
— BUCKMINSTER FULLER (Contemporary)
Nine Chains to the Moon

WHAT does it mean to be sick? If you still believe in atoms
and accept matter as your personal god, you will probably
maintain that sickness is the result of some causative agent
which invades your body. In that event you will then seek a
remedy which will destroy or neutralize the offending agent.
Many see human illness as a malfunction in a 'machine', an
isolated, skin-encapsulated sack of organs. It's just as likely
that disease represents the suffering of a divine spark trapped
in a morass of matter, trapped by attachment, to an illusion.
We don't know for sure. All we have are theories. Examining
the theories, we select one and decide 'I believe'. We stake
our lives on those beliefs.

If, for instance, you found a lump on your body, would
you consult a surgeon? A psychic? An astrologer? All three?
Whose advice would you follow?

The Surgeon General of the United States has noted
that "A growing number of people, faced with a diagnosis of
cancer, are turning to treatments like Laetrile, faith healers,
and even prayer. The major hazard of these approaches,"
he says, "must be considered the diversion of patients from

conventional, proven therapy." As the nation's chief health official, the doctor worries about patients who turn to these unorthodox methods, "only to find out too late that their treatments are ineffective." Why do you suppose so many people are doing that? Why would anyone with a devastating, often fatal condition turn away from conventional, proven therapy and risk his or her life by embracing unorthodox methods, especially if — as it is said — they are ineffective?

One possible reason is the fact that many people have the notion that conventional cancer treatment, consisting of surgery, radiation, and chemotherapy (the ingestion of cellular toxins), is often mutilating, debilitating, and expensive. They are right. It often is. Many would prefer to take their chances with the disease rather than undergo the horrors of treatment and then be faced with the disastrously ruinous cost. Consider the comments on 'the health cost crisis' as reported in *Newsweek* magazine.

"The American people have reached a point of outrage with the way hospital costs have increased," reports Joseph Califano, secretary of the Department of Health, Education and Welfare. A Bethlehem Steel executive says, "I find it absolutely mind-boggling that an industry this size operates almost immune to the forces most basic to our economy." The concept *health industry* implies that health is something you have to *buy,* like oil, or sugar, or coffee. Health is seen as a commodity, to be sold for the best market price obtainable. What is it we buy in our quest for health? "A vastly expanding . . . and expensive . . . technology that has made medicine more of a science and less of an art in recent years," says the magazine *Newsweek.* How much does all this cost us? Suffice it to say that the overhead cost of auto workers' health insurance adds more to the price of a new car than does the cost of the steel. There is another factor, perhaps even more significant than cost, in our current health care controversy.

"We have lost something in the areas of human relations, compassion, and communication." So says Max Parrott, M.D., past president of the American Medical Association. "This loss is a consequence of our highly developed technology, and is most evident in large institutions." Dr. Parrott identifies himself as a primary care physician, out in the field, serving individual people. This, he feels, differentiates him from the specialists who practice only in large institutions. These individuals, he believes, ". . . tend to confuse service with function. Routinization, standardization, and emphasis on productivity may help the busy specialist and the institution, but too often the patient feels that some basic need has not been met."

Conventional cancer treatments, using highly sophisticated, complex, and expensive instrumentation, must be delivered in institutions. You can't, for instance, make a house call with a scanning electron microscope in your bag or carry a cobalt bomb around in your car. "As with any institution," warned the AMA spokesman, "there is danger of infection with the bureaucratic virus — the virus of not caring."

Routinization, standardization, and emphasis on productivity are the means by which industry markets a commodity with maximal efficiency. "Industry," said the late Dr. E. F. Schumacher, "always wants to eliminate the human factor. If we find that natural raw materials still have too much of the cussedness of life in them, we prefer synthetic materials. Faced with this awkward factor, the human factor, we choose automation." Compare this with Dr. Parrott's admonition that "What happens to the patient is so individualized that the practice of medicine must be kept flexible." Automation is not always compatible with flexibility.

This point is crucial to our discussion. Medical specialists and large institutions are geared to deal with the average situation, the unfoldment of a specific disease in a hypothetical patient. Faced with its singularly unique unfoldment or course in a specific individual, they attack the disease—ignoring the individual patient and Sir William Osler's admonition that "It is much more important to know what sort of a patient has a disease than what sort of disease a patient has." Specialists proceed 'according to the book'. Technologic treatment of disease processes constitutes the science of medicine. Ministering to sick humans is called the art of medicine.

"It's often been said," observed Dr. Parrott, "that the technical aspects of medicine are easy. The difficult part is dealing with the personality of the patient, the so-called psychological or human factor. This takes up a great deal of the time of the practicing physician. It is harder on the doctor's constitution than all of the technical aspects of medicine. It may even cause his or her demise in the case of a physician with an autonomic nervous system that can't take the heat."

Human beings, however, are too unpredictable and individualistic to permit the promulgation of rigid rules regarding the manner in which they are to be 'managed' when they become sick. The compulsively technological health professional would like to type your symptom complex into a computer, and have the computer respond like a multiple-choice soda machine, popping prescriptions for the proper pills. Steadfastly thwarting the dream of total automation is this difficult living factor—'the human factor'—the psyche of the patient.

People are like snowflakes: no two are alike. The difference between what one person may do with a set of symptoms as compared with another is unbelievable. How one patient may respond to a particular treatment program has nothing to do with what may happen in the next case. Penicillin, for instance, may cure a fulminating pneumonia in one person and send the next into intensive care with a totally unexpected allergic reaction, perhaps taking a life in a case where it was offered as a cure.

"Flexibility, adaptability, and sensitivity to personal needs," says Dr. Parrott, "characterize the art of medicine, which must constantly temper and complement the technology of medicine." Recall the comment in *Newsweek* which suggested that the health industry today is selling "a vastly expanding—and expensive—technology that has made medicine more of a science and less of an art." Public resentment of this trend can be measured in terms of the sharp rise in malpractice suits. We must remember, however, that the health industry arose, grew, and prospered out of the best intentions and with the wholehearted support of the American public.

A malpractice lawyer, Jerry Green, has examined the currently explosive health issue as it appears in our judicial system. "Why," he asked, "are so many people hauling their doctors into court?" Answering his own question, he continued, "The failure of doctors to live up to the kind of expectations nurtured by their patients—that's the connecting thread in all the cases, the underlying root cause for the breakdown in doctor-patient relationships. When you compare these expectations with what doctors are trained to do, you uncover the basic misunderstanding."

I remember what they taught me in medical school. They taught me how to combat disease. I learned about pathologic processes, classified them as disease entities, and studied the weaponry and technology available in our medical arsenal. Then, as now, there was very little instruction in what my father used to call 'the art of dealing with the public'.

"People go to doctors because they want to feel good," observed attorney Jerry Green. "Doctors, for their part, feel that they are entering into a contractual agreement for the management of some pathologic condition or other. The patient is saying, 'My life isn't working, these are my symptoms, put it right.' "

Responding to the patient's plea for help, the specialist answers, "Bring me your disease, your limb, or your liver. Take your personality, your psyche, to a psychiatrist. I will recommend one if you like." It's easy to see how this misunderstanding winds up in court. The highly trained, pathology-oriented, extremely busy specialist could be compared to the transmission man in an auto repair shop, who has no interest in how home or job tensions affect your driving. "Bring me your transmission," he might say, "take your personal problems to a psychologist."

Actually, all these specialists might be perfectly wonderful people. Even if they do care about you as a fellow human, they simply aren't trained to deal with the most intimate, personal aspects of your problems, and in large, busy medical complexes, they don't have the time to make the attempt. They are trained to efficiently perform a technological rather than a humanitarian service. If you should seek this service from a psychiatrist or psychologist, you will probably find that they, too, are scientifically trained, disease-oriented, and frequently pharmaceutically inclined.

And yet, if the physician has done everything exactly the way it was taught at medical school, and the patient doesn't improve, whose fault is it? "The bulk of society today," says Jerry Green, "wants what it sees on television. People want to get up in the morning, have an instant breakfast, take a pill to wake up and stay alert, then come home and take another to make them drowsy so they can fall asleep." From the physician, they want some instant medicine which will protect and preserve them from the consequences of modern society's estrangement from nature and from the body. "It's time we took responsibility for our own health," he adds.

There is an implicit contract between physicians and

patients. As I see it, physicians and patients are engaged in an unintentional conspiracy — a conspiracy to suppress symptoms. Members of the health industry — the drug companies, manufacturers of sophisticated medical hardware, and hospital complexes — merely supply the tools. The current contract between patient and physician calls for the removal, eradication, or suppression of the patient's symptoms using the finest and most modern technology available.

How does that work in practice? Suppose that I, a family doctor, make a house call to see a patient with a pain in the gluteus maximus — the buttock. In the course of my physical examination I find that the patient is sitting on a tack. Were I to honor the implicit contract which postulates symptom suppression as the primary objective of my visit, I might administer a quarter grain of morphine, write a prescription for codeine pills, and leave instructions to call me in the morning. The morning report might be something like, "As long as I take the pills, it doesn't hurt, Doc." In a few days, the pain medicine loses its effectiveness. Time and increasing dosage bring two new developments. The symptom suppression stops and side effects begin to appear. Symptoms may now include nausea and vomiting along with pain in the buttock. Faced with apparent failure of the drug approach, I might recommend surgery. There are varying surgical solutions to the problem. I could sever the nerve which carries pain sensations from the buttock to the spinal cord, or I could perform a dorsal root rhizotomy. That's a highly specialized neurosurgical operation where we cut the sensory nerve as it enters the spine. Alternatively, we could freeze the thalamus in the brain, the structure which is thought to be the body's pain center. I might send him or her to a pain control center where a group of specialists would give instructions on how to live with pain. As a last resort, I might suggest a prefrontal lobotomy, after which there would be pain, but the victim wouldn't notice it. If I suggested getting up off the tack, the response would likely be, "But Doc, I make my living sitting on tacks."

Ridiculous? Yes. Uncommon? No. Think of a professional athlete with a knee injury, a factory worker with low back pain, an executive with an ulcer, or a housewife with arthritis. All such people demand eradication of symptoms which are brought on or aggravated by their means of earning a livelihood. Few people see pain or suffering as a message telling them to take a hand out of the flame or to get off a metaphorical tack.

Insofar as we see health as the victorious outcome of a war of annihilation against germs, viruses, tumors, and other invaders, we are likely to overlook the role played by our own habits, thinking patterns, and belief structures. I wonder how many of us are ready to let go of the picture of patient as victim — caught between malevolent microorganisms on one side and an avaricious health industry on the other. Are overpriced hospitals and doctors who won't make house calls actually depriving you of your right to health?

It does little good to attack the health industry or the doctor business. An industrial corporation is an artificial person whose primary purpose is the accumulation of profit. Emphasizing standardization, routinization, and productivity, a corporation is by nature prone to a deficiency in ability to serve the individual needs of each customer. Think about it for a moment. If you contract with a medical corporation to have your gall bladder removed, who's to blame if your human needs go unsatisfied?

A folk tale illuminates the point. A frog was about to cross a river when she was hailed by a passing scorpion. "Would you please carry me across the river on your back?" he asked nicely. "Don't be ridiculous!" the frog replied. "You're a scorpion, and scorpions sting."

"I promise not to sting you, love," he crooned, arching his back. After much persuasion, she reluctantly agreed, allowing him to crawl onto her back. Halfway across the river she felt the scorpion's stinger plunge into her body. "You crazy thing!" she screamed. "You promised! Now we'll both die!"

"I know," he murmured as they began to sink, "I can't help myself. I'm a scorpion, you know."

As the Duchess in Lewis Carroll's *Alice in Wonderland* said, "Tut, tut. Everything's got a moral if only you can find it."

Moral: If you get stung buying health from a corporation, who's to blame?

2 / Patient, Heal Thyself

"The art of medicine consists of amusing the patient while nature cures the disease."
— VOLTAIRE (1694–1778)

WHAT IS IT you want from your doctor when you're sick? Do you demand symptom suppression, or guidance toward a state of health and well-being? Do you expect that someone will fix your ailing body as a mechanic fixes a malfunction in a machine? Have you ever considered the possibility that you could do it yourself, that you could influence your own state of health? Perhaps if you were aware of the power and efficiency of your body's defenses, you might be willing to trust them more. Let's see how effective they can be against something really serious, like cancer.

"If we can discover how to activate the immune system, we may have a successful way to fight cancer." This dramatic announcement appears in a report entitled "Immunotherapy and Cancer," authored by Dr. J. L. Krahenbuhl of the highly respected Palo Alto Medical Research Foundation and Dr. J. S. Remington, professor of medicine, Stanford Medical School. The report examines orthodox medicine's approach to cancer, that which the Surgeon General calls 'conventional, proven therapy', and tells us why orthodox therapy is losing favor.

"Currently," say Drs. Krahenbuhl and Remington, "we have three weapons against cancer: surgery, radiation, and chemotherapy. *All three are radical treatments with fundamental shortcomings* [italics mine]. . . . For years scientists have searched for a way to direct the cancer patient's own defenses against the disease. Many believe that this rediscovered form of cancer treatment represents a fourth major weapon in fighting cancer."

The 'fourth major weapon' is something within the patient — within you. It is known to science as the *immune defense system* — your body's natural ability to repel invasion. The implications go far beyond treatment of cancer. We're talking about your inborn ability to defend yourself against germs, pollutants, foreign substances, or tumors — the inborn ability of the body to heal itself.

Many people are unaware of the fact that they are not helpless in the face of disease. Invaded by a virus or threatened by a germ, they turn to the doctor, to the scientist, and to the health industry for help, for the know-how and the weaponry to combat what is viewed as a malevolent force which has invaded the body. This represents the strategy of 'attack and destroy'. Directing the patient's own defenses against the disease represents an alternative tactic. Let's compare the two approaches.

The human body may be treated as an ecosystem, an ecological unit. The best way to deal with an alien life form which threatens the ecosystem is the introduction of a natural enemy, an organism which feeds on the invader and harms nothing else in the environment. Technology provides techniques which usually destroy life indiscriminately, the useful forms as well as the harmful.

Suppose, for example, you had gophers in your garden. How would you get rid of them? An attack-and-destroy person might lace the soil with poison, perhaps arsenic or strychnine. The fundamental shortcoming of that approach is that you might accidentally poison your pet, a small child, or perhaps even yourself. In a like manner, chemotherapy's cytotoxins (cell poisons) and radiation therapy destroy normal cells along with the cancer cells. Thus, patients often notice that they vomit a lot, their hair falls out, and they feel generally awful. Surgery, the third and last weapon in our conventional armamentarium, also presents a fundamental problem. Cutting away the localized mass of tumor cells, one opens blood vessels. This affords the wildly growing malignancy direct access to the bloodstream, the royal road to every corner of the body. Only one mutant cell needs to get through to start a metastasis, a beachhead in the lung, liver, brain, spine, or wherever.

Moreover, let's assume that, after using a combination of all three assault tactics, ninety-nine percent of the growth is destroyed. For every million malignant cells present before the onslaught, only ten thousand would survive. That's more than enough to seal the patient's fate. Using orthodox attack-and-destroy procedures, the patient is sometimes mortally wounded. "The side effects of radiotherapy and chemotherapy," say Drs. Remington and Krahenbuhl, "can seriously restrict the patient's ability to mount an immune response." We bomb our own troops, so to speak. Let's look at a viable alternative — another way.

The Immune Response — Mobilizing The Defenders

About seventy-five years ago, Dr. William B. Coley, a physician practicing in New York, decided to try a new strategy in his battle to save the lives of cancer victims. He would get his patients to fight back! There was a theory making the rounds at that time which seemed to offer some hope. A scientist named Metchnikoff had observed specialized cells from the human body which demonstrated the ability to devour and destroy alien substances as well as invading life forms. This observation led him to formulate the concept of *cellular immunity*.

Perhaps, reasoned Dr. Coley, Metchnikoff's defender cells could be induced to attack tumors. With this in mind he concocted a potion that later became popularly known as 'Coley's Toxins'. Injected into a cancer patient, the mixture induced chills, fever, and all the classic symptoms of acute bacterial infection — and it also made tumors shrink! In some cases, the cancer recurred. *In many, there was no recurrence even after decades.*

Dr. Coley has provided strong evidence to support his hypothesis. If you can get the body's defenses mobilized against one invader (germs), they will at the same time attack another, such as cancer. Your ability to defend yourself is natural to your being. It's in your blood.

Blood, as you may know, is essentially a solution of saltwater. Like the ocean, your bloodstream teems with swarms of tiny living beings. Blood cells, as some of these little creatures are called, come in two basic colors, red and white. Red blood cells (RBCs) carry the breath of life, oxygen. White blood cells (WBCs) repel invasion by foreign bodies or by alien life forms. There are three kinds of WBCs with names as colorful as they are descriptive. *Polymorphonuclear leukocytes,* or the 'white shape changers', formed in the bone marrow, attack and destroy invading organisms on a one-to-one basis. In hand-to-hand combat, so to speak, the shape changers engulf and digest the invaders. Fever, chills, and a generally rotten feeling mark the battle raging within your body. Accumulation of the corpses of the heroic little shape changers gives pus its characteristic color.

How do the shape changers, or *polys*, recognize an invader? After all, germs don't wear uniforms. They do it the way you recognize a rotten egg in a rose garden — by the smell. Just as your nose knows the scent of a rotten egg, your blood cells sense and interpret the chemical coatings on the alien. Antigens, which may be called chemical 'smells', activate defender or immune cells just as kitchen odors alert a fastidious housekeeper. Responding to the introduction of a new 'smell', or antigen, certain white cells, the *lymphocytes*, manufacture and release *antibodies*.

An antibody is an exact reflection of the antigen. Chemically, the antibody zigs where the antigen zags. Released by the millions from the sturdy little lymphocytes, antibodies pour into your bloodstream, avidly seeking their mates. Think of unbridled lust and you get a picture of the intensity of their quest. Meeting in the bloodstream, the two unite like pieces of a jigsaw puzzle. Poisonous to the invader cell, the antigen-antibody combination has its own unique chemical structure or 'smell'. (Marvel at the intricate beauty of your body's adaptive mechanisms, and consider how little we trust them.)

When we immunize children against diphtheria, for example, we inject inactivated germs which have lost most of their potency yet retain their smell (antigen). Responding to this scent, the immune system releases hordes of antibodies, more than enough to deal with the immunizing challenge. The surplus antibodies hang around in the child's bloodstream year after year, hunting the smell of antigen. Should infection take place, the response is quick, efficient, and specific. Uniting with the bacterial antigens, the circulating antibodies fix themselves tenaciously and permanently to the hapless invaders, poisoning them as they attract the deadly white shape changers.

"We have acquired evidence that there exists a cytotoxic [cell poisoning] lymphocyte population whose effect is in its ability to recognize and interact with antibody molecules that coat the surface of the target cells." Reporting this discovery is Dr. J. C. Cerottini, associate professor of immunology, faculty of medicine, University of Lausanne, Switzerland. Two classes of cytotoxic lymphocytes are described: *Cytotoxic T lymphocytes* (CTL), the cell poisoners, and "K" or *killer* cells. The cell poisoners have the ability to search out and destroy cells bearing a specific antigen odor. The killers attack and annihilate alien life forms bearing the antibody.

People who recover from measles or mumps are usually immune for life. Activating the defense system through immunization procedures, we have eliminated smallpox and sharply curtailed polio. The work of Metchnikoff suggests the mechanism for these phenomena — the patient's own immune system — a most effective weapon against these deadly infections. The experiments with Coley's Toxins suggest that the immune system, alerted by one invader, will attack others. Injecting patients with cowpox virus, for example, renders them immune to the deadlier smallpox virus. The two pox viruses smell alike. The work of Krahenbuhl and Remington, cited earlier, supports the hypothesis embraced by Dr. Coley, that an aroused immune system will destroy cancer cells. Why does a challenging dose of Coley's Toxins make cancer masses shrink? "Working with animals and certain types of human cancer," write Krahenbuhl and Remington, *"researchers have discovered antigens on malignant cells that may also spark the immune system."* (Italics mine.) Some cancer cells have an odor!

Krahenbuhl and Remington theorize that, in order to survive in the human body, the cancer must somehow mask its antigen or the immune system must be inactivated. There are killer lymphocytes circulating in your blood right now which have the ability to find and eliminate mutant or malignant cells. Scenting the antigen of a cancer cell, some lymphocytes attack it directly. Others secrete antibodies which attach themselves to cancer cells and attract the killers. Still others secrete chemical messengers which activate yet another defense system, the *macrophages* — the 'great eaters'. Activated macrophages do not limit their aggression to the invader which first aroused them. Once aroused, they will indiscriminately destroy any and all aliens in their path. Provoked by a germ, a macrophage will, as Dr. Coley showed clinically, attack cancer cells and then devour the debris. So voracious are they that, placed on a dish, they will attempt to eat the glass. Macrophages do not attack normal body cells.

The *immunosurveillance theory* holds that we make cancer cells constantly, but that they are systematically apprehended and eliminated by the immune system. *Why does this system sometimes break down?* Why do the defender cells allow cancer to run rampant and unchecked through the body? Here we have reached the border of the agreed upon, the edge of the unknown. Proceeding further we run into a thicket of theories.

Some think the trigger is a grief reaction. Depression slows down all bodily processes, including the immune system, they theorize. Others believe it's a subtle form of suicide, a bodily response to an 'I wish I were dead' attitude. We have evidence that cancer may be provoked by the air we breathe, the foods we eat, or by the pajamas our children wear to bed. Since it is clearly almost impossible to avoid contact with known cancer causes, the most important questions become: *How do we stimulate and strengthen our resistance? How do we activate the immune system?*

Conventional, orthodox medical technology offers us little hope. "Progress will be difficult," say Krahenbuhl and Remington. "Serious hazards are associated with the administration of living organisms or their toxic by-products.... Vaccination against cancer remains only a distant hope.... An enormous amount of basic research remains to be done before immunotherapy can be understood and fully exploited." Chances of recovery from some forms of cancer are no better today than they were seventy-five years ago. For the cancer victim, time is short and the need is great.

So people turn to unconventional treatment methods, like Laetrile, faith healing, and prayer.

Reporting on the Laetrile controversy, a CBS-TV documentary film showed a person shaking with righteous indignation, complaining about "a bunch of bureaucrats taking away my freedom of choice! If I want to try unorthodox methods," went the argument, "I damned well will! I don't want anyone interfering with the decisions I make about my own body!" The announcer noted that some courts have agreed with this contention. They have found that it is not okay for the federal government to send people to jail for aiding and abetting the use of Laetrile in place of or in addition to surgery, chemotherapy, and radiation.

Are those who opt for Laetrile doomed, as the Surgeon General says, "to find out too late that their treatments are ineffective"? What is the experimental evidence? How can we be sure that Laetrile doesn't cure human cancer? The CBS documentary reported that some people say they have tried Laetrile and recovered from cancer. Dr. Ernesto Contreras, who heads the Clinica Del Mar in Tijuana, Mexico, told a television audience of thirty million Americans that he has over one hundred cases indicating clinical cure or significant improvement in cancer patients receiving Laetrile. While opponents of Laetrile from the camp of orthodox medicine dispute these claims, Laetrile's defenders just as staunchly challenge the results of laboratory experiments that purport to show the controversial extract's ineffectiveness against cancer.

The procedure for testing a drug's anticancer potential is relatively simple. Tumors are artificially induced in laboratory animals like rats, mice, or guinea pigs. Laetrile is then fed or injected into the creatures and researchers observe the responses of the tumors. According to government scientists, Laetrile did nothing to stop or inhibit tumor growth in test animals. Furthermore, they observed that live cancer cells in a solution containing the substance continued to thrive and divide rapidly.

In my opinion, that series of experiments is pretty persuasive evidence that Laetrile does not affect the course of tumors *which have been artificially induced in laboratory animals.* These findings in no way contradict Dr. Contreras's claim that in his experience injection of Laetrile has been followed by arrest and destruction of spontaneously occurring tumors growing in living humans. It's important to realize that laboratory test animals may not, in all cases, respond to the administration of therapeutic substances in the same way that humans do.

The results are perfectly compatible. There's nothing to argue about. Everybody is right. We need a simple, rational concept, a hypothesis which will account for all the data. Admitting that remissions do occur in many cancer victims using unorthodox methods, Food and Drug Administration scientists offer an interesting and, in my opinion, valid theory. "The reason so many patients feel better after taking Laetrile," says an FDA spokesperson, "is the psychological lift they get from being treated by people who have a strong stake in their getting well. Another major factor is the belief that the substance will work." Caring along with the curing, grace along with the gadgetry, and faith in the remedy seem to produce results where technology alone fails. Evaluating the evidence submitted by both sides, we may now construct an operating hypothesis: *There is a factor found only in humans which, in conjunction with Laetrile, may induce the destruction of malignant tumors.* That's our old friend, the human factor — the psyche of the patient.

Can the psyche, the mind, activate the immune system by an act of will — or faith? Perhaps it can. Some people can walk on hot coals and not be burned. Others trained in yoga techniques learn to take command of their autonomic nervous systems. Using biofeedback techniques, patients learn to control heart rate, blood pressure, and other 'involuntary' body functions. It is obvious that the psyche can by an act of will alter the behavior of bodily structures, aggregates of atoms in space. You need only move a finger to prove that fact.

The simple ease with which the human body performs intricately coordinated movements in space is largely taken for granted. Yet the almost incredible dexterity of the hands and fingers of a violinist or of a concert pianist reminds us that training and practice are the key. Consider, in comparison, the clumsy movements of the newborn — arms and legs reaching, jerking, threshing around in the crib, eyes diffuse and unfocussed. You couldn't always command the neural circuitry of your body the way you do now. How did you learn?

Consider that as an infant you were unaware of any separation between yourself and your environment. Recall the primal experience of hunger. You experienced pain: disease. At first you grasped, you screamed, squirmed, and, aah, salvation — the magical materialization of milk from a mother's breast or from a bottle. Warm, nourishing fluid flowed into your burning belly. Peace, ease, and comfort were restored. You were healed! You learned to reach out with exquisite accuracy to grasp the bottle or breast that brought an end to your suffering. Then you learned to hold the bottle by yourself — a triumph of neuromuscular coordination. Later, you learned to hold a spoon and convey food with more or less accuracy into your mouth. The fact that some of the food ended up on your cheeks, chin, bib, the floor, in your hair — and sometimes in your mother's hair — is characteristic of the awkward beginning stages in learning a new skill. The important thing is, you learned to deal with hunger pains. *You learned to heal yourself*.

Later, you achieved voluntary control over the activities of the bladder and the bowel—a prodigious mind-over-matter feat. Why stop there? The electrochemical circuits in your wise old brain are designed to coordinate and maintain *all* bodily functions. You may as well learn to use them to deal with other sources of pain and distress. As long as you have the option, why not give it a try? You may get a bit of egg on your chin at first, just as you did when you were a baby, and you may find that you are increasingly able to hit the target.

Current scientific research, especially in the field of psychosomatic medicine, and my own experience with patients as a family practitioner indicate that just as we learned to make a fist, we humans can learn to control symptoms of physical disorders. We have the means, we need only learn the method.

When you were squeezed out of the womb onto the terrestrial plane, you weren't thrown out empty handed. In order to facilitate your journeys over the face of the earth, you were equipped with an exquisitely sophisticated, incomprehensibly complicated guidance system: a functioning human brain. Your brain never sleeps. It hums away day and night, whether you're asleep or awake. It runs your body and shapes your reality. It is commonly accepted that most people use only ten percent of the brain's capacity. We are just beginning to learn how to use the other ninety percent. This discussion is about using that other ninety percent.

Our human brain makes available to us some thirty trillion separate circuits. Consciousness (that part of you which is using your eyes to read this book as it commands the hands to turn the pages) programs brain circuitry to impose its will on the physical body. You use your body more efficiently as you extend control of your psyche over more and more brain circuitry. If you learn to control enough brain circuits, perhaps you can activate your own immune system should the need arise.

The activating factor, Dr. Parrott's 'human factor', *the psyche,* is usually relegated to the realm of the 'soft sciences' (psychology and psychiatry) by scientists who subscribe to a strictly 'objective' approach to medical research. At the other end of the spectrum we find a growing number of scientists whose pioneering research points to the psyche as the single most important factor in creating health or sustaining suffering. In the pages which follow we will be taking a closer look at some examples of that research as we further explore the role of the psyche in the management of disease and in the alleviation of suffering.

3 / Healing Is Believing

"Man is made by his belief. As he believes, so he is."

— Bhagavad-Gita

BELIEF is basically a function of the psyche. I have suggested that removal of the distorting lens of rigid outworn belief structures can reestablish the healing connection. What is the evidence to support this hypothesis?

In its *Second Report on Alcohol and Health* (1974), the United States Government published research statistics revealing that moderate drinkers are likely to outlive teetotalers (including ex-drinkers). This contention is supported by the work of Arthur L. Klatsky and his colleagues at the Kaiser-Permanente Medical Center in Oakland, California. Investigating the background of 464 heart attack victims, they discovered that an inordinately large proportion were non-drinkers. In a follow-up study of 120,000 patients, they found that moderate drinkers were thirty percent less likely to suffer coronary occlusion than were their steadfastly sober counterparts. Another six-year study by Katsuhiko Yano and associates in Hawaii was consistent with the findings of Klatsky's Kaiser-Permanente group. Among those who suffered heart attack, a fatal outcome was more frequently observed among non-drinkers than drinkers.

Apparently alcohol can play a beneficial role in the health and well-being of some people. How does it work? A theory advanced to account for these findings postulates that perhaps alcohol interferes with the deposition of cholesterol and fats in the walls of the arteries. This may be so, and there is another possible explanation.

Morris Chafetz, former director of the National Institute of Alcohol Abuse and Alcoholism, suggests that alcohol protects the cardiac patient by reducing anxiety, relieving pain, and promoting relaxation. Thus we see that an important effect of alcohol is its action on the psyche. Alcohol and other psychoactive (mind-altering) substances dissolve usual thought and behavior patterns. Tensions and job worries diminish or disappear, and for the duration of the altered state of consciousness, life takes on an easier and mellower aspect. The rational thinking mind fades into the background, giving way to a more intuitive and emotional appreciation of the life environment. Now, I'm not talking about habitual excessive abuse of alcohol, but moderate use of this mind-altering substance. Excessive use seems to aggravate and amplify distress as it creates new problems. Yet even moderate ingestion of alcohol and the accompanying fadeout of rational thought processes are regarded with ambivalence in our society, which venerates reason with a fervor approaching the religious.

Rationality seems to be regarded as the elixir of sanity and social responsibility, the prime requisite for acceptable, predictable, 'self-controlled' behavior. Certain that everything has a rational explanation, we mistrust attitudes based primarily on intuition, faith, and other nonrational modes of knowing. I'm not knocking the obviously beneficial aspects of rationality, but I would like to suggest that habitual excessive indulgence in 90-proof rationality can be just as harmful to our health as any other compulsive addiction, such as overeating, drug abuse, or alcoholism. It might even do us in before our time.

The problem with rational, thinking mind — the sound-less, chattering thought machine — is that it's a creature of the past. That's its limitation. But the square pegs of the past don't always fit the round holes of the present. Rational mind doesn't deal well with the unexpected and the un-explained. Faced with the irrevocably unreasonable, the persistently paradoxical, the fuses of the rational mind some-times blow out, plunging us into the darkness of distress, anxiety, and confusion.

Yet events are unreasonable and people are paradox-ical. The unexpected and the out-of-the-ordinary lie at the cutting edge of the unfolding life process. Blind adherence to icy rationality represents a form of *rigor mortis,* a death-like rigidity in the face of life's continual rebirth and re-newal with each sunrise.

The unexpected and the unexplained are commonly associated with the word *paranormal.* Consider the posi-tion taken by the Committee for the Scientific Investigation of Claims of the Paranormal. The Committee consists of a group of scientists and science writers investigating "the growing belief in astrology, UFOs, the Bermuda Triangle, and other cults of unreason." Defining paranormal as "un-proven or mystic phenomena," the committee warns us that "belief in such things can harm or even kill people." I suppose that's true. Perhaps belief structures, rigid ideas about how things are, *can* kill. I know a specialist who feels that the thing which is killing his cancer patients is the be-lief that they have an incurable disease. Yet belief can and does play a positive role in health as well. Take the belief in the power of the pill, for example, the relatively mild concoctions sold over the counter in drug stores. Of these, aspirin is by far the most widely used. It is considered by many to be the single most useful drug in our mighty medi-cal armamentarium.

Many people take aspirin to relieve headaches, muscle cramps, or joint pains. Others swallow aspirin when they feel a need to calm down. Some take it at bedtime because they say the drug helps them fall asleep. Now, as far as we know, there is nothing in the structure of aspirin which has tranquilizing or sedative properties. We notice that aspirin reduces pain and makes swollen joints feel better. We can only theorize about the mechanism. A recent article in the press reported that males who take four aspirin daily experience fifty percent fewer heart attacks. The blood platelets seem to become slippery so they don't stick together to form clots inside the heart's nutrient vessels. What is the mechanism for these miracles? What part is played by belief in the power of the pill?

If someone were to say that concealed within the bark of a white willow tree lies a mystical herb with power to ease pain, extend life, bring peace to the soul and sleep to the body, many people would dismiss the information as the jabberings of a cultist. If that same someone used different language, if they told you that whenever they need to calm down or fall asleep they take aspirin, and it works like a charm just as it does for headaches, you might even try it yourself should the need arise. If I told you that salicin — a close relative of the active ingredient of aspirin — is found in the bark and leaves of the white willow, you might see for yourself the way in which we arbitrarily reject much useful information because of language and prejudice.

Aspirin is a truly mystical substance. We can mimic nature. We can reproduce the structure of the healing herb, turn it into a chemical, and roll it into a pill. Yet we have never solved the mystery of the means by which aspirin manifests its healing magic. Maybe its mode of action is partly psychological — 'in the mind'. If so, perhaps we have seriously underestimated the therapeutic capabilities of the nonrational aspects of the psyche.

When we consider the many extraordinary effects people associate with a simple substance like aspirin, effects that go beyond the known pharmaceutical properties of the substance, we begin to get an inkling that beliefs and attitudes play a larger role in healing than we may have heretofore suspected. Once again we encounter Dr. Parrott's 'human factor', that mysterious aspect of human nature which seems somehow to be involved in the etiology and the alleviation of dis-ease and dis-comfort.

If we postulate that the human factor — the psyche — controls the off-on switch that activates the body's natural immune system, then we are impelled to have a look at that class of phenomena called 'mind-over-matter' events. Until recently, most scientists and medical researchers have steadfastly refused to seriously consider such phenomena. Mind-over-matter events have been dismissed as mystical, occult, or paranormal, not proper subjects for scientific study. Interestingly, that attitude has begun to change, partly as a result of new research, partly because of a fuller understanding of the conceptual framework within which science operates.

For the moment, let's adopt the scientific method, the detached attitude scientists apply when examining new hypotheses and data. This method requires that we suspend preconceptions, beliefs, and prior opinions. We must take a nonjudgmental, openminded perspective toward the information we're checking out. Let's survey the hypothesis that at least some mind-over-matter events might be true, just to see where it takes us.

One can only be healed, some say, by chemical compounds — drugs, pills, or injections. Yet medical literature dating back to the time of Hippocrates is replete with clinical case histories concerning people who have been healed by statues, stones, and saints, as well as by chemical compounds. Patients successfully treated by all these methods universally report the subjective sensation of healing energy entering their bodies, followed by clearing of their symptoms, alleviation of their suffering.

Suppose you were bitten by a rattlesnake. Where would you seek healing? In biblical times, Moses is said to have built a serpent of brass, and those who were bitten by poisonous snakes needed only to look at it to be saved from death. I once listened to a radio talk-show in which the host was discussing *snakestones*. Snakestones are rare and expensive stones which are said by believers to induce healing in cases of snakebite. "Frankly," said the announcer, "if I was bitten by a rattler, I would opt for a shot of antivenom unless I was out in the desert or some other remote area. Under those circumstances, I'd sure be willing to give the snakestone a whirl." The talk-show host was inclined to base his primary choice on the method most familiar, effective, and reliable *within the cultural context of his experience.* An eminently reasonable attitude. We might assume, similarly, that an American Indian or an Israelite of ancient times would prefer the snakestone or brass serpent as the treatment of choice—opting for a shot of antivenom (assuming it were offered to them) only as a last resort, and only if they were told that the antivenom was a remedy accepted by another culture.

How would you feel after being struck by a rattler as you watched your doctor fill a syringe with life-giving serum? Would you not experience ease, confidence, and a feeling of relief? Imagine, then, the feelings of the Indian or Israelite—one as he clutches his life-giving amulet, the other as he gazes upon the serpent of brass. How would you describe that feeling? Salvation? Bliss? Overwhelming gratitude?

There's another aspect to it. The doctor empties the syringe into your vein. Seeing and feeling that event, you sense a powerful new force in your body, in your very blood. The same sense of infusion of a beneficial healing force most likely ran through the veins of the Indian, the Israelite, and those healed by saints.

Can an inert object, the snakestone, be as effective as a modern magic potion such as antivenom? The answer for you might be 'no'—unless you found yourself trapped in the desert with snakebite, forced by circumstances to choose between certain death and faith in the workings of the snakestone. A compulsively rational person would have problems. His or her belief system might interfere.

We believe, for example, that medical researchers have studied the effects of snake venom on the human body and, understanding its *modus operandi,* have devised counter- acting serums which act to block the harmful effects of the poison. That's what we were taught in school, and we may have read newspaper accounts about snakebite victims be- ing rushed to hospitals where they were saved from death by administration of the appropriate antivenom. In court, evidence like that would be thrown out as hearsay, second- hand information. I'm not saying it isn't reliable informa- tion, I'm only pointing out that, for most of us, our faith in chemical compounds such as antivenom is based on pure hearsay. The native American Indian and the Israelite held other beliefs about the functioning of the human body and how healing took place, and the snakestone, the serpent of brass, fit as well into their belief systems as antivenom in ours. How do we choose?

You swallow the pill, submit to the injection, gaze at the brass serpent, or rub the stone. Observing the results, you notice that either you heal or you don't. Then and only then can you be sure of the efficacy of your favorite nostrum or remedy. Are all our approaches to human disease and suffering merely rituals? What, if anything, do the touch of the stone, the sight of the brass serpent, and the prick of the needle have in common? Is it possible that they are all trig- ger mechanisms inducing an alteration in body chemistry to manifest the desired healing? Is the psyche the agent which pulls the trigger?

The Placebo Effect

In an article from the *Saturday Review* titled "The Mysterious Placebo — How Mind Helps Medicine Work," Norman Cousins writes, "This strange sounding word *placebo* is pointing medical science straight in the direction of something akin to a revolution in the theory and practice of medicine." A placebo is a sugar pill, a saltwater injection, or other substance which is in itself completely inert pharmaceutically. It can't cure, kill, arrest, or change anything — on its own. "Take this medicine," says the doctor, "it'll fix you right up." Does fake medicine work as well as the real thing?

Let's look at some of the experimental evidence. Reviewing the literature, author Cousins finds that "Today, the once lowly placebo is receiving serious attention from medical scholars." Researchers know the placebo as a dummy pill or shot that looks exactly like the real medicine.

Since placebos can evidently generate chemical changes within the body, even though they are pharmaceutically inert, our hypothesis that "at least some mind-over-matter events might be true" begins to take on substance. How can the psyche trigger a chemical reaction? A bulb lights when electricity flows through it. The 'on' switch does not *create* electricity. Pull a chain, press a button, or throw a switch, and bulb glows with light. Ingest a chemical, pray for divine intervention, search your psyche, and your body glows with health. Is the healing process something we simply 'turn on'?

The placebo effect brings us back to the human factor — the factor which ignites the healing process. Rituals like rubbing the snakestone, laying on of hands, or prayer may also trigger the placebo effect. It seems reasonable to wonder about the extent to which the placebo effect plays a role in the response of the human body to pharmaceutically active drugs as well as phony pills and injections.

"Medical investigators," writes Cousins, "are reporting evidence that the placebo, in a large number of cases, not only looks like a powerful medication, it *acts* like a potent drug! They now regard the placebo as an authentic therapeutic agent for altering body chemistry and for helping to mobilize the body's defenses in combating disorder or disease," continues the *Saturday Review* article. Recall the statement of Krahenbuhl and Remington with regard to activating the body's immune system: "For years scientists have searched for a way to direct the cancer patient's own defenses against the disease. Many believe this rediscovered form of treatment represents a fourth major weapon in fighting cancer." The others, as previously mentioned, are surgery, radiation, and chemotherapy. Can placebos activate our defenses against disease?

Dr. H. K. Beecher of Harvard evaluated the placebo's effectiveness against pain. Administering placebos instead of morphine to post-operative patients, he found the placebo to be seventy-seven percent as effective as our most potent available painkiller. Probing further into the powers of the placebo, Dr. Beecher collected findings from fifteen studies involving about eleven hundred patients. All had received placebos instead of active drugs for a wide range of medical complaints. He found that thirty-five percent of the patients treated by placebo experienced satisfactory relief of symptoms. Complaints included pain, dizziness, headache, cough, and simple nervous tension.

Arthritis is usually treated with aspirin and cortisone, sometimes with gold. We are not certain about the mode of action of these substances. We just know that they work, so we use them. Are they all placebos? Magical pills and potions? Consider the results of a study in which eighty-eight arthritic patients were treated exclusively with pla-

Placebo's Easing Of Pain Studied

LOS ANGELES (AP)—Sugar pills masquerading as medicine sometimes produce dramatic results because they can trick the brain into producing a natural pain-killer similar to morphine, scientists said Monday.

University of California researchers said they have solved the long-standing medical puzzle of why a placebo — a sugar or salt solution that, by itself, does nothing — eases pain in about one-third of all patients.

That fact usually is dismissed as a purely pshchological reaction, something that is "all in your mind." But Dr. Howard L. Fields said the University of California-San Francisco study proved otherwise.

He said that in many patients the placebo somehow triggers the release of pain-fighting chemicals called endorphins.

"The fact that you get relief [from a placebo] depends on your expectation of getting relief so to that extent it may be psychological. But the pain suppression is real," Fields said in a telephone interview.

The study, which was outlined in Montreal Monday during the Second World Congress on Pain, suggested dramatic new directions in the study and control of pain.

Fields said he and his coworkers, Drs. Jon Levine and Newton Gordon, conducted the experiment with 50 dental patients who had teeth pulled a few hours earlier.

He said about one-third of their test subjects reported decreased pain after being injected with a placebo. But the benefits of the placebo uniformly disappeared following injection of a substance that blocked the action of morphine and related drugs.

The injection had no effect on those who were not helped by the placebo, he said.

Endorphins are the best explanation for those results, he said. The self-produced pain-killers were identified just three years ago and little is known about how or why they are produced.

WASHINGTON POST 8/78

cebos. Eighty-eight other patients, the control group, received conventional antiarthritis therapy. The number of patients showing improvement was the same in both groups. "Some of the patients who had experienced no relief from the placebo pills were given placebo injections. Sixty-four percent of those given injections reported relief and improvement," claimed the report. Defining 'relief and improvement', the report states, "For the entire group, the benefits included pain relief, general improvement in eating, sleeping, and reduction in swelling."

Norman Cousins once asked Dr. Albert Schweitzer to explain witch-doctor cures. "He said that I was asking him to divulge a secret that doctors have carried ever since Hippocrates." Dr. Schweitzer offered this illuminating observation: "The witch-doctor succeeds for the same reason all the rest of us succeed. Each patient carries his own doctor inside him. They come to us not knowing that truth. We are at our best when we give the doctor who resides within each patient a chance to go to work."

The human factor is the doctor who resides within. The placebo effect is that doctor's healing magic. We find that trust and belief are essential elements in the transformational process we call *healing. Trust and belief are functions of the psyche.* Many people have difficulty visualizing how a psychic function, human consciousness, can alter the behavior of physical matter in space — the body — so they don't even try. Let's examine the basis for this difficulty.

PART II
Reality Reconsidered

"The real voyage of discovery consists not in
seeking new lands but in seeing with new eyes."
— MARCEL PROUST (1871–1922)

4 / Atomism to Holism

*"It is not that things are illusory, but their sepa-
rateness in the fabric of reality is illusory."*

—ANONYMOUS

WHAT KEEPS US from activating our efficient immune systems to deal with particular diseases? Why can't we turn
on the switch right now, if need be, to initiate the healing
process? We can—if we'll take the trouble to examine our
personal belief systems, our opinions and shoulds, and remove those that stand in the way of recovery. The human
biocomputer—the brain—is programmed to reject new in-
put that conflicts with existing beliefs, at least until we stop
identifying with those beliefs. Let's look at some current
theories about the human body, matter, and the universe
to see how they may affect our experience of health and
disease.

The notion that disease is caused by the entry into the
body of tiny, imperceptible particles was expressed by the
Roman encyclopedist Varro as early as 100 B.C. This view
was picked up again by Frascatoro in 1546 and by Athanasius
Kircher and Pierre Borel about a century later. But it was
the work of Louis Pasteur (1822–1895) that gave rise to the
science of bacteriology and catapulted the notion that things
cause disease into the modern Western mind.

Thus, strictly empirical health scientists rigorously avoid consideration of what Dr. Parrott calls 'the human factor' and proceed on the basis of hard-line objectivity, searching for entities like germs, viruses, and other material agents that are said to cause disease. Hopefully, they feel, new drugs, therapies, and surgical procedures can be found to specifically combat or eliminate each individual disease entity. It is important to note that this view entertains the idea that *things* cause disease, things that invade our bodies like armies cross borders. And things, we are told, consist of matter, which in turn consists of atoms.

What about our psyche? Everyone seems to agree that a human being consists of both mind and body. Mind and body, psyche and soma, consciousness and matter. This is the split you experience when you say 'my body'. What animates your body? Now, I'm not talking about the nervous system, electrochemical impulses, or any intermediary systems. I'm asking what *originates* movement in the body. The psyche, your consciousness, your mind, we might say. Where is that—in the body? The body animated by your psyche is composed of matter, isn't it? What *is* the matter?

The Matter of Things

The idea that all matter is composed of atoms is the brainchild of a Greek philosopher named Democritus who lived over 2,000 years ago. Looking around one day, having nothing better to do, he wondered how small a thing could be and still be called a *thing*. If, for instance, you smashed a building down to a pile of bricks, then crushed a brick into fine debris, you'd end up with sand.

With your mind, break up a grain of sand into the smallest pieces imaginable. If you think like Democritus (and most of us do, since that's what they taught us in school), you'll wind up with an imaginary pile of the smallest 'things' there are—only this time you'll call them *atoms* or subatomic particles.

Now, no one has actually seen an atom, least of all the Greek philosopher who invented them. He was just playing a mind game. He wasn't even a scientist. But Democritus was a man with an idea whose time had come, so to speak, for the Greek intelligentsia of that period (circa 400 B.C.) had become fascinated with speculations about such impractical things as the nature of reality. The theorizings of Democritus (sometimes called 'the laughing philosopher') were recognized, recorded, and revered along with the later works of Plato, Aristotle, and other Greek philosophers who have so heavily influenced Western thought.

Atoms, Democritus postulated, are purely passive, devoid of life, unconscious, indivisible, and without intelligence. The tiniest nubbins of anything that can still be called things, atoms were placed on earth by the gods. These same gods then sent down *spirit* to animate and direct these little atom-pellets of matter. Spirit pushes and moves atoms around much as wind moves the leaves of trees. Modern scientists call this spirit *energy,* another term borrowed from the ancient Greeks.

For hundreds of years after the decline of the Golden Age of Greek culture, the atoms of Democritus slept in some obscure pile of dusty manuscripts, perhaps in an ancient church or monastery. Then, mysteriously, they reappeared in a sixteenth century treatise by the famous Copernicus, the astronomer who removed the planet Earth from its central location in the solar system and sent it spinning — along with other planets — around the sun. Atoms again popped up in writings by students of Galileo, the staunch defender of the Copernican system, but dropped back to sleep while the ingenious Sir Isaac Newton revolutionized science in the late seventeenth and early eighteenth centuries.

The immense success of Newtonian classical mechanics prompted imitation by medical and biological scientists, who somewhat naively assumed that simple mechanical models of complex living organisms would lead to the same magnificent breakthroughs Newton had achieved. In some cases, it's fair to say they did. But in many other instances, the disregard of life by mechanistically-inclined life scientists led them only down blind alleys.

After Galileo's students' brief flirtation with atomism, the nubbins created by Democritus took another three-century nap until awakened abruptly by such nineteenth-century researchers as Pierre and Marie Curie, Dalton, Thompson, Avogadro, Mendeleyev, and others. The hunt for the ultimate nubbin was on again, this time with a vengeance. The criticisms of Austrian physicist Ernst Mach (1838–1916), who cautioned his contemporaries that atoms were only abstractions, "economical ways of symbolizing experience," were ridiculed or ignored. The protagonists and their language have changed since then, but the theme remains the same. Thus we are told that buildings may be made of individual clay bricks, that the human body is made of isolated cells, that both bricks and cells are collections of atoms, and that atoms themselves are ultimately composed of myriads of subatomic particles. But where is life in this scheme of things?

The cornerstone of the Newtonian method and of modern science is experiment, observation, and measurement. Since life is not a measurable entity, it disappeared in the subsequent development of the physical sciences. The great Newton himself was not blind to the loss. In his *Scholium Generale,* Newton wrote about "a most subtle spirit which pervades and lies hid in all gross bodies; by the force and action of which ... all sensation is excited and the members of animal bodies move at the command of the will." His contemporaries and later scientists largely dismissed such writings as eccentric nonsense. Many still do so today. This amputation of the psyche leaves a gaping hole in our theoretical structuring of reality.

The Mysterious Vibrating Particle

Under the microscope, the living cell is seen to be made of separate granules called *cytoplasm*. The big difference between a grain of sand and a granule of cytoplasm is that the latter seems to move spontaneously. (Atoms within a grain of sand are also said to vibrate, but their movement is constrained by bonds within the crystalline structure; a grain of sand doesn't move when viewed through a microscope.) Energy operates with a significantly greater degree of freedom within the granule of cytoplasm than it does within the grain of sand. We call this greater degree of freedom *life*. What makes the isolated granules of cytoplasm inside a living cell move? What makes your body move?

Democritus, some scientists, and most orthodox Western theologians state that it is the Spirit of God, Newton's 'most subtle spirit', contained within the granules, the cytoplasm, and your body. Other scientists peer through their microscopes and talk about 'metabolic processes' or 'electrochemical reactions'. What does that mean? What makes living things move? We simply don't know. Experts all agree that the spontaneously gyrating granules of cytoplasm are 'alive' as they divide the territory into different conceptual categories. Thus we find life and spirit discussed by theologians and philosophers, energy and matter by physicists, cell structure and function by biologists. This diversion spawns disputes like: Which came first — energy or matter? The structure or the function? The motion or the granule? The chicken or the egg? Heal the arbitrary division and we resolve the dispute.

'Energy', 'function', 'motion', and 'chicken' all represent a single concept: the concept of *action*. On the other hand, words like 'matter', 'structure', 'granule', and 'egg' suggest passivity, *inaction*. Here we have four pairs of opposites. Let's try to fuse a pair of these opposites and see what happens.

Fusion of opposites sparks release of energy. Joining the positive to the negative, scientists released electromagnetism — and created our modern technological civilization. Fusing oppositely charged ions, we make molecules and compounds, "creating a better world through chemistry." Among living creatures, fusion of the opposite sexes creates an autonomous unique life form with an irrepressible urge to evolve — like you, for instance. The particular fusion or re-connection we're after is accomplished by answering the question, "What happens when an irresistible force meets an immovable object?"

With his dazzlingly brilliant formula, $E = MC^2$, Albert Einstein solved the koan, fused the opposites, and released the energy of the atomic age. The formula suggests that *the granule of protoplasm is a crystallized form of the energy which makes it move.* Newtonian physics claimed that things may *have* energy; Einsteinian physics says that things *are* energy.

Let's be clear on what that means, in terms of both its relation to current scientific theory and its potential effects on you. If you truly believe, deep inside, that disease entities are 'things' and that your body consists of a collection of lifeless, inert molecules, atoms, subatomic particles, and quarks, then you are probably caught up in the notion that both the cause of disease (germs, for example) and its effects on you (feeling sick) are beyond the influence of your mind. Mother Nature simply chalked up her cue stick, slammed the cue ball into a configuration of pool balls (germs) as you were walking by, and the eightball (one of the nastiest germs in the game) happened to land in your side pocket. Bingo! You're it, the accidental victim of a purely random chain of cause-and-effect events. Is that view true for you? If so, you're still caught up in the old morass of matter, cause, and effect, with a slight dose of atomic misunderstanding complicating your case. There are, of course, endless variations of belief systems that block the healing work of the human factor, the psyche. Some people shrug off illness with an attitude of resignation: "I suppose it's God's will," or "I haven't been taking care of myself recently." Such attitudes suggest severence, states of separation—self from God, mind from body, cause from effect. One part of the self is amputated from another part of the same self. Again, such beliefs are tied to the view of isolated entities interacting like billiard balls in cause-and-effect chains. Current scientific theories and research do not support such beliefs.

According to the reasoning of Democritus, the vibrating granules of the cells of our bodies are made of atoms. Physicist Niels Bohr has suggested that the atom consists of a relatively motionless nucleus containing protons and neutrons, surrounded by a shell of wildly gyrating electrons, like planets spinning around the sun. Now, no one has ever seen a proton, neutron, or electron. Just as some people see tracks in the snow as evidence of 'Bigfoot', scientists see tracks in a cloud chamber as evidence of subatomic particles. Like atoms before them, subatomic particles have been billed as 'the ultimate building blocks of matter'. The ultimate building block of the ultimate building block is said by some to be the quark.

What is a quark, an electron, or an atom? "Isolated material particles and abstractions, their properties being definable and observable through their actions on other systems," answers Dr. Niels Bohr. The word *quark* is a nonsense word devised by author James Joyce in his work *Finnegans Wake*. He invented it to make the phrase 'Three quarks for Muster Mark' rhyme. It would seem to be a perfectly appropriate term for the ultimate abstraction of the ultimate abstraction.

Scientists use abstractions to describe and organize data derived from experimental observations. They do not, themselves, claim the abstractions *are* the reality. Neither should you. The map is not the territory. A mistake like that could endanger your health or undermine your well-being.

Unlike "all the king's horses and all the king's men," helplessly confounded by Humpty Dumpty's fall from the wall and the resulting disarray of broken pieces, we may now begin to reassemble our quarks, atoms, and granules of cytoplasm into whole living bodies.

5 / Shifting Paradigms

"There are more things in heaven and earth, Horatio, than are dreamed of in your philosophy."
— W. SHAKESPEARE , (1564–1616)
Hamlet

THOMAS S. KUHN in his work *The Structure of Scientific Revolutions* observed that scientific progress has taken place historically through a series of shifting paradigms. A paradigm is a map or blueprint of reality, not the reality itself. A paradigm consists of a set of theories, mathematical formulas, and hypotheses which describe the structure and behavior of a particular portion of reality in terms of the known information about that reality. Basically, a paradigm is a tool for further understanding our experience. Just as we wouldn't eat the cookbook for the dinner it describes, we shouldn't mistake the paradigm for the reality it represents. Just as we throw away old recipes when new favorites are found, science abandons obsolete and outdated paradigms.

For example, the Newtonian paradigm, which once beautifully seemed to account for what was known about physical systems, was displaced by the Einsteinian paradigm. Why? New data had been discovered, and the new ingredients couldn't be cooked according to Sir Isaac's old recipes. The speed of light had been measured, blackbody radiation didn't make sense, radioactivity and the photo-electric effect had been discovered. The new data didn't fit the old theories. It was time for a new model of the new reality. We may now be experiencing the beginnings of a paradigm shift in the health sciences under the impetus of medical research and new data drawn from her sister sciences.

Paradigm shifts are not simple processes. Each shift is marked by a period of sharp debate, relative confusion, and often severe antagonism between opposing groups of scientists. When scientists first encounter data that doesn't fit the old theories or formulas, they either ignore it or plug a new hypothesis into the leak in the old belief system. But the finger-in-the-dike approach can't prevent the dam from bursting as new discoveries and data create additional leaks, exposing increasingly major faults in the old paradigm.

Although at that point the old system may be recognized as falling apart, the lifeboats aren't launched until a new paradigm is invented by some handy genius. Then the younger scientists, particularly, are the first to make the switch, followed by all but a handful of the old guard. A few stalwart loyalists hang stubbornly onto the old paradigm until they die. Even scientists tend to grow attached to their belief systems, procrastinating over change, perhaps mistaking their abstractions for that piece of the real universe mirrored in their theories. "No Trespassing, Private Paradigm," the sign in their minds might read.

Actually, the useful portions of the old paradigm are generally incorporated into the new one. Einstein's formulas on relativity, for example, reduce to Newton's formulas at speeds significantly slower than the velocity of light.

It's also important to realize that science isn't isolated from its social surroundings. The repercussions of a scientific revolution shake society, just as a social revolution can bounce science around. The Newtonian revolution was accompanied by, and perhaps helped stimulate, the overthrow of the European feudal system and the medieval social paradigm—a way of life. The industrial revolution that swept Europe and the United States was, in a sense, a stepchild of the Newtonian revolution. The notion that things are isolated entities interacting in cause-and-effect chains replaced the ancient idea that things are purposeful, interrelated in a 'great chain of being'. It seems to be no accident that the new view was so remarkably well adapted to the emerging social systems of both science and industry.

Our modern health industry, with its Newtonian heritage, has experienced its share of triumphs and failures in the course of its evolution. But the emergence of data that doesn't fit signals that change is in the air. Research centered around the human factor has begun to haunt the hallowed halls of modern medical science as the rusty machinery of the cause-and-effect paradigm seems to squeak, falter, and to seriously limit further progress in our understanding of health and disease.

In one of my previous books* I cited experimental evidence which suggests that the human brain, your brain, has access to records of sensory information that are independent of what you experience. That is, what you see out there in the real world is as much a projection of your paradigm, what you expect to see, as it is a perception of some objective reality which is actually there. In the previous chapter, we explored the notion that certain beliefs about the structure of matter—including the human body—can be harmful to your health. We've taken the universe apart down to atoms and quarks. Now we're going to put it back together again.

The great theoretical physicist Max Born once wrote,

Time, Space, and the Mind (Celestial Arts, 1976).

"Matter as given by our senses appears as a secondary phenomenon, created by the interaction of our sense organs with processes whose nature can be discovered only indirectly through theoretical interpretations of experimentally observed relationships. [I see something in my environment — I touch it and it feels solid.] To designate the result of this operation by the old word 'matter' seems to me wrong." Why is it wrong? What's amiss in calling apparently solid collections of atoms matter? — or things?

Fritjof Capra, theoretical physicist and author of *The Tao of Physics,* observes, "At the atomic level, solid material *objects* of classical [Newtonian] physics dissolve into patterns of probabilities. These patterns do not represent probabilities of *things,* but probabilities of *interconnections.* We see the universe not as a collection of physical objects, but rather a complicated web of relations between the various parts of the whole." The scientist ogling nature through his machines is one of the parts of the whole. Physicist Werner Heisenberg put it this way: "Natural Science does not simply describe and explain nature. It is part of the interplay between nature and ourselves." *The very act of observing changes the nature of that which we observe.* Dr. Capra sums it up: "The electron does not have objective properties independent of my mind . . . *there are no things* . . . the chain of cause and effect ends in the consciousness of the observer. . . . The fact that we speak of an 'object', an electron, proton, or neutron, suggests that we have some independent physical entity in mind, which is first prepared, and then measured. In the framework of quantum mechanics, the concept of a distinct physical entity can be defined precisely only if this entity is infinitely far away from the observer. In practice this is, of course, impossible." Observer and observed fuse into a single event. That fusion has exploded and transformed our notions of reality — our paradigm.

According to quantum physics, subatomic particles are

not matter, but energy waves of varying frequencies that interact to create the *illusion* of matter. The effect of energy vibrating at different frequencies coincides with our sensory perceptions of solids, liquids, and gases — as well as heat, color, and sound. Our sense organs experience 'waves', our intellect creates 'things'.

Your physical body, the thing you bring to the doctor for repair and overhaul, is, at its basic core level, not a fixed structure or a static thing. It is a process, a constant state of changing and becoming. Alan Watts observed, "A living body is not a fixed thing, but a flowing event — a flame; a whirlpool." Neither the flame, the whirlpool, nor the body have definite borders.

Vanishing Borders

As we move from atomism toward holism, we notice that a change takes place. The border lines separating independent, isolated entities have begun to grow hazy and indistinct. It's like traveling from Europe to America, where state borders are marked by signs rather than by barriers and guards. Crossing the great Atlantic Ocean, sailing eastward, Europeans entered the New World. The American continent as we know it today did not exist for its first European inhabitants. They knew only an immeasurably vast, unknown wilderness without borders or other divisions. Science's elimination of the border between the observer and the data being observed catapults us into the same vast unknown. Arriving at full-fledged holism, we find that the comfortable compartments, cubicles, and categories in which we stored and sorted myriads of isolated facts and concepts are useless. The differentiating walls have melted, allowing our most cherished concepts to run together and comingle. Let's look at some examples.

I think it would be safe to assume that many of my readers are certain that *places* are different from, and not the same as, *time*. Organizing the way they experience their environment or reality, many mentally place space and time in separate, hard-edged conceptual compartments. The notion 'downtown', for example, is in a different category from and unrelated to the notion 'three o'clock' according to this way of thinking.

Modern scientific thought no longer distinguishes between space and time, preferring instead to talk about a single entity called *space-time*, or, more specifically, 'the four-dimensional space-time continuum'. A continuum is a seamless undivided whole.

With this in mind, if someone asked you to describe what it's like downtown, you would have to tell them that downtown at three o'clock in the morning is not the same as downtown at three o'clock in the afternoon, and that both are quite different from downtown during rush hour. Impressionist painters like Monet and Alfred Sisley hinted at the intimate relation between time and space when they showed that a scene painted in morning light was quite different visually from the same landscape painted in mid-afternoon. Any native will tell you that New York City is not the same place in December as it is in June. A particular place or space can only be described accurately in terms of time.

The same is true for time. What was yesterday like? In order to answer that question, I would have to know whether the querent was interested in learning about yesterday on Mars or about yesterday in Brooklyn.

Just as physicists and mathematicians have eradicated the illusory border between place and time, biological scientists are now telling us that it is impossible to understand or to describe the behavior of a life form, a living *thing*, unless one studies it in its natural environment—the *place* in which it lives. Time, organism, and environment must be studied as a unit. Thus we find the illusory borders between separate sciences like geography (the description of places) and biology (the study of life) fading as they blend and coalesce within the broader science of ecology.

Think about the implications for your own personal day-to-day life. What does the elimination of discrete borders by the hard sciences mean to you? Consider the notion that the relationship between your body and your environment might be the same as the relationship between your mind and your brain. One couldn't exist without the other. They are parts of a single, interconnected system. The entire universe, according to modern science, is a field, a continuum. The archaic notion that the collection of atoms, the pile of matter which you call 'my body' is somehow walled off from other discrete piles of matter called 'things in the outside world', has been challenged. Recall Dr. Heisenberg's statement that science is part of the interplay between nature and ourselves. In a basic sense life itself is that same interplay.

Elimination of the barrier (the differentiation between the observing scientist and the observed data) makes untenable and obsolete one of our most common and most entrenched illusions — the concept called *objective reality*. The theory that there is a real world outside of and separate from my physical body is illogical. It is also obsolete — it has outlived its usefulness. If the observer and the observed entity are a unit, a single system, how is it possible to separate yourself from the universe you're studying so you can be objective? How can you, a living creature, an integral part of nature, separate yourself from nature in order to study her 'objectively'?

Why should there be a border between your psyche and your body, or your body and your environment? They are part of one single event, you. A living human organism is, like the Christian God, simultaneously a trinity and a unity. A single phenomenon with three aspects. Your psyche, your body, and your environment are facets of a single unified process with no boundaries, a process you call _____ (insert your first name). They are all aspects of one single event. If you realize that your immediate environment is an integral part of planet Earth, you can begin to see the entire universe as contiguous with your psyche through your body. At the subatomic level, reality is now seen as a unified field, a continuum. That's how modern physics describes it. In this view, we are not isolated entities competing against an alien environment — we are interconnected, one vast organism, not unlike the 'Ancient of Days' described by the Kabbalah.

Science provides for us a matrix of facts, theories, and data which is internally self-consistent and logical. We take this for knowledge. Out of a particular matrix we may construct a paradigm, a pattern which helps us order, interpret, and enjoy our experience of living. A new reality paradigm seems to be emerging, as the 'facts' now being reported by scientists are found to be bursting the seams of the old matrix. Since we can't throw out the data, we must revise our paradigm, our belief structure.

Like Dr. Thomas S. Kuhn, space scientist Carl Sagan notes, "The most fundamental axioms and conclusions may be challenged; the prevailing hypotheses must survive confrontations with observation.... The history of science is full of cases where previously accepted theories and hypotheses have been entirely overthrown, to be replaced by new ideas which more adequately explain the data. [Recall the paradigm shift from 'the world is flat' to 'the world is round'.] Proponents of a prevailing belief, if they are incapable of defending it, are well advised to abandon it," says Dr. Sagan.

Proponents of 'the domino theory of reality', the cause-and-effect paradigm, believe that the stuff we perceive with our five senses is the real world, the ultimate and only true reality. Our sense organs perceive differences in a flood of impinging sensory stimuli—our minds create a world of things consisting of separate and differentiated objects. Operating on a figure-ground principle as described by Gestalt psychology, our minds define artificial boundaries within a homogeneous sea of stimuli. These relatively arbitrary margins set off *things* or *objects* against a background of boundless, infinite space. In the world of Newtonian physics, the world of borders, every thing is different from everything else: the meow is somehow different from the cat, the wave is different from the sea. A self-consistent matrix which explains only itself is taken for knowledge of ultimate reality. As philosopher William James suggests, we think we have seen directly into the mind of God, and discovered there some absolute truth.

Just as the Greek philosopher Democritus structured matter out of discrete, isolated atoms, we tend to structure experience out of independent, disconnected events. Thus many people still hold the belief that concepts like time, space, energy, and matter are descriptive of discrete, disconnected phenomena. This world view, I have suggested, might be named 'the domino theory of reality'. The dominoes represent atoms, particles of matter which are inert and devoid of intelligence, sensation, or purpose. Continually bumping into each other in an endless chain of mechanical causes and effects, atoms are supposed to move in time through space, impinging on my psyche from outside in the form of *phenomena* (objects and events). Proponents of the domino theory of reality maintain that events are different from things—that both originate outside the psyche which merely experiences and reacts to them. Do you believe that? Psychologist Dr. Jean Houston suggests that "concept louses up percept." What I believe distorts what I perceive.

Modern science tells us that the border between events and things, energy and mass, is permeable if not illusory. If I can't actually demonstrate a border between me and something which I experience as not-me (my psyche versus my typewriter), I can't logically and reasonably presume that such a border exists. Ancient Eastern philosophy tells me, "Thou are that!" Modern quantum physics and field theory suggest that the observer (my psyche) and the observed (my typewriter) are a single event. If I accept this view, I change the way I experience the world. I inhabit a different universe.

Peering through the closeup lens of subatomic physics, scientists have dissected the diamond we call 'the real world' and found that, in the words of Dr. Fritjof Capra, "There are no things." I asked Dr. Capra how this notion (that at the subatomic level we find no things, only 'probabilities of relationships') affected his personal moment-to-moment existence. He replied, "Not at all. While this is true at the subatomic level, it is not practical on the daily level." Dr. Capra presumes that things like buses exist, and that if one hits him, he will be killed or injured. He is, therefore, careful to stay out of their way. A useful operating hypothesis.

We can at one level keep the domino theory. We need only see through the illusory barrier separating the psyche from objects and events. We would do well to consider the evidence that the 'ring around the psyche' which prevents us from initiating our own healing processes is an illusion, a sort of hallucination. The ring is removed by considering that *the chain of cause and effect begins and ends in the psyche*. Perhaps I flick the first domino with my psyche, thus becoming the first cause of all the circumstances and events in my life.

The holistic paradigm suggests that psyche, body, and environment are one. There are no borders. Einstein pulled the plug on the domino paradigm when he observed that adoption of a frame of reference which is moving at velocities approaching the speed of light forces us to change the equation sets by which we describe the universe mathematically. At slower velocities, we, along with Dr. Capra, can rely on the older Newtonian guidelines and concepts to keep from getting run over by busses. But as rocket ships and television cameras hurtle through space, we notice that the world takes on a different appearance. Compare the picture of Christina's World with the view from outer space. Christina's World, the world of the five senses, is not the ultimate reality. It is a tiny portion of the reality which reveals itself to us as our rockets achieve escape velocity and our TV cameras look back at the world from the surface of the moon.

Our view of the universe is changing — and with that new view, we are beginning to experience a magically different universe.

When astronaut Neil Armstrong set foot upon the lunar surface, the eye of humanity, the color television camera, flashed back to Mother Earth a vision of herself, a vision never before beheld by the eyes of mortal man. We saw our beautiful blue planet suspended in space, floating in an endless sea of blackness — the universe. Where were the borders between nations, the teeming billions of individual, isolated atomistic people? They had vanished! It's all a matter of perspective.

ANDREW WYETH
Collection The Museum of Modern Art, New York

Christina's World (1948)

PHOTO CREDIT: NASA

6 / Ring Around the Psyche

"The center is still and silent in the heart of an eternal dance of circles."
— RABINDRANATH TAGORE (1861–1941)
Fireflies

THE REAL WORLD, the outermost layer of our living experience, is the endless infinity we call the universe, endless and infinite whether we magnify it with a microscope or peer at it through a telescope. Imagine yourself as the navigation officer of a spaceship. What would you do if you received instructions to plot an immediate course to the center of the universe? How would you solve that problem?

Think about that for a moment, then, for the fun of it, run through the following exercise.

1. Focus your attention on the point inside your skull where light from each eye and sound from each ear converge.
2. From this point, think of a sphere expanding outward to infinity.
3. Fill the sphere with stuff we'll call *space-time,* 'space' when it's still and 'time' when it flows.
4. Add an ample supply of magic creation dust, which invisible in itself, can accumulate to form 'things' in the infinite space-time sphere.
5. Call this thing-making stuff 'atoms', 'quarks', 'mindons', or whatever you like.

6. Look around, and there you are — at the center of the universe....

7. Thinking things....

Any point in an infinite system is the center of that system. Each of us is that center.

In my book *Time Space, and Mind,* I mentioned a decision by the California Supreme Court in response to a lawsuit brought by a group of parents who objected to the purely materialist concepts of the origin of the Earth and its life forms taught by the public schools. When the parade of witnesses finished their testimony, the court decided that neither the 'big bang' cosmologists, the 'survival of the fittest' biologists, nor the protagonists of Biblical creation had proven their arguments according to the rules of evidence. Given that decision, it is just as likely that our world was created by an all-powerful being with a long white beard as by a cosmic explosion followed by an accidental accumulation of mindless matter. That's what the public schools have to tell your kids if you live in California. No one has definitely proved how our world came about in the first place. All we have are theories, and your theory may create your reality.

Look out at the sky some night and find the Big Dipper. Realize that each star is a sun, like ours or perhaps larger. The stars that make it up are separated by eons in time and light years in space. It's entirely possible that some of them aren't even there any more! The light entering your eyes originated at different times — yet you still see that beautiful constellation. Have you ever considered that the Big Dipper may be a gigantic optical illusion — an illusion that only exists when you look at it?

The ability to fuse separate events in space and time into a hypothetical entity called a *constellation* is a function of your innermost being, your central core — your psyche.

How do you suppose the Big Dipper looks to your dog? Or to the mosquito buzzing around your ear? We normally assume that the dog, the mosquito, and other observers, like the constellation itself, exist independently and are somehow disconnected from each other and from ourselves. In his book *Spectrum of Consciousness,* author Ken Wilber suggests that this is the means by which we ourselves create the phenomena of space.

If I am 'here' and that is 'there', Wilber suggests, the stuff in between must be empty space. Within that space, we may identify other objects. Having in this manner created space and things, we make some decisions about our relationship to those creations. We decide that they are outside, that they are somehow 'not me'. This decision is an amputation, a dismembering. Cut off from the rest of reality, the decider's identity shrinks and becomes limited to the boundaries of the physical body. We become, in the words of Timothy Leary, "skin encapsulated egos."

In the course of a religious experience, under the influence of drugs, or during a totally engrossing activity, we may re-member. Spontaneously we recapture the feeling of unity, at-onement with the universe. At the center of this inconceivable vastness, reaching from the realm of subatomic mind particles called quarks through the black holes in outer space into other infinite universes, is that divine spark, your psyche.

The *Oxford English Dictionary* defines the psyche as "The animating principle in humans and other living beings.... The source of all vital activities — rational or irrational ... as distinguished from body or mind." In ancient Greece, the term *psyche* was used in much the same sense as *soul.* Greek mythology tells us that Psyche was once a woman, so lovely that people praised her beauty and virtues above those of the goddess Aphrodite. Angered, Aphrodite sent her son Eros, the god of love, down to earth to take revenge on the innocent Psyche. Eros, stunned by the Earthling's charms, fell in love with Psyche instead and made her his bride. Perhaps the association of beauty and virtue with love (the creative principle) accounts for the evolution of the word *psyche* in language to mean "the animating principle," the "source of all vital activities."

Considering the relations between psyche and body, the eminent Swiss psychiatrict Dr. Carl G. Jung wondered in 1928 whether "the psyche can be looked upon as a relatively closed system." The concept of the psyche as a closed system can be compared to the concept of the 'involuntary nervous system'. This idea implies that there are parts of the human body that can't be brought under voluntary control. Conscious mind and physical body in these areas are held to be separated by some mysterious impenetrable barrier. If the psyche, one's most central self, were a closed system, then the only connection between a flu patient and the influenza virus would be that they simultaneously inhabit the same space-time vehicle — the human body. Consistent with this widely accepted hypothesis, people are said to be unable by an act of will to alter or affect the course of organic disease. But we've already reviewed evidence that people *do* affect the course of organic disease — the placebo effect. Let's have a closer look at this 'ring around the psyche' notion to see if we can shed some light on the problem.

Imagine that you are a volunteer in a sensory deprivation experiment. Eyes occluded by lightproof patches, ears stuffed with soundproof wadding, you step slowly into a tank of tepid water until you are floating, in weightless isolation. Like a narcotic drug, sensory deprivation abolishes all external sensation. The subjective experience is not unlike that of undergoing general anesthesia. Reality seems to fade into oblivion. For a few moments, there may be a feeling of panic. Then you remember you are safe; you are being watched by the staff, so you allow yourself to sink into black nothingness.

The silence may last for only a few moments, but while it is there, the experience is one of pure, pristine awareness, the living awareness of the psyche at the center of your being.

Then, silently, stealthily, thoughts appear. "What on earth am I doing here? Why did I ever volunteer for such a stupid experiment?" Empty awareness is disturbed. "Right now, I could have been at the beach [at home, at a party, and so on]." Images come, floating by as imagination takes you where you might have gone, to do what you like to do. Associations trigger changes of scene. Memories and emotions drift past. Consciousness creates images (holograms) to replace the stimuli which usually enter from the world of things 'out there'. (One can, of course, reproduce the hallucinations or holograms by another means, by going to sleep and creating dreams.) Notice at this point that your psyche has become surrounded by layers of thoughts, emotions, and visions—like layers of an onion.

Where do you go when the dream ends? Where are you when there are no external or internal stimuli to capture your attention—no thoughts, images, or emotions to indicate to you your own existence?

Nowhere! Like Jonah in the belly of the whale, you inhabit an empty space. There at the center of the silence, at the vortex of the void, lies your quintessence like a point within a circle. Capable of love as well as hate, joy as well as despair, your truly essential self knows only emptiness. In this state you are all-powerful, omnipotent . . . like a deity.

Suddenly, you give a start as you feel yourself being touched, then helped from the sensory deprivation tank. The ear wadding is removed, you hear sounds, people-noises, a voice gently telling you your time is up. And then there is light. The blindfold is removed. You find yourself seeing people, things — objects — the fifth layer of the onion. The psyche, your quintessence, once again experiences itself at the center of a circle layered with things, emotions, thoughts, and dreams.

Slipping back into your clothes, your personality, and your belief structures, you sally forth into the 'real world'. Which is the 'real you'?

Consider the myth of Narcissus in the light of our discussion. This tale in its various forms has been kicking around the literature for perhaps two thousand years. We humans don't keep anything that long unless it's of some value to us. Myths are not mere fairy tales, but psychological models meant to tell us something about ourselves. They reflect aspects of our daily lives.

Narcissus was a beautiful god who had never seen himself until one day when he happened to peer into a pool of quiet, still water as he stooped to drink. Believing, as many of us do, that his being was limited and bounded by the skin of his physical body, he presumed that he was gazing at a creature who, like the pool that reflected it, was separate from himself. Hopelessly enamored of his own reflection, he leaned over to embrace his love, fell into the pool, and drowned.

In this allegory, the god Narcissus is you. He represents the most essential part of your being, your psyche — that metaphysical aspect which perceives things, thoughts, emotions, and dreams: your consciousness, if you will.

Recall for a moment what it feels like to awaken from a deep, dreamless sleep. For an instant, or two, maybe longer, you may not remember where you are or what you're about. We enter time-space in the morning, as we do at birth, without the limitations of job, family, beliefs, opinions, or shoulds. For a while we are omnipotent, able to do anything. Then our memory tapes engage: We get up, brush our teeth, and begin our usual daily routine. We gaze into the pool of life, fall in, and drown. Narcissus is you, transformed from the god-like state of omnipotence and empty awareness into the ego-trapped state wherein you think you actually *are* your physical body, your thoughts, your emotions, or your occupation.

Every day we have a conscious, living experience, and each night it shuts off. After expanding into a physical body and through it, into time-space adventures, we begin to tire and lose interest. Our attention retreats into the confines of the body and the mind, finally leaving both as we enter the deep unconscious (in non-REM sleep). We sleep, perhaps we dream . . . and have another conscious living experience, an out-of-the-body conscious life experience — which shuts off as we swing back through the mind toward consciousness within a body inhabiting a world, living a life, a 'real' life. How do we make sense out of all this? The evidence at hand suggests that memory plays a key role in pulling us into the pool.

Memory Tapes

"Memory is above all the mechanism that makes us creatures of time. Without it, we would live in an eternal present unmarked by anxiety over past or future," says Tony Jones, editor of *Quest* magazine. Memory is the yoke to which we bind our vital energies. Attachments are links in the chain which imprisons our free, universal spirit — our evolving consciousness, our psyche.

"And that's not all of it," continues editor Jones. "Memory also holds us in, caught in our own frame of reference." Perhaps sickness is a signal from the psyche to your mind, its way of shedding some light on the need to change your frame of reference: to free you and itself from an obsolete, decaying structure. Think of the snake shedding its outworn, constructing skin, or a bird destroying the encasing matter of the eggshell, a shell which once protected and nurtured, but which now restricts and suffocates. Let's consider the work of neurophysiologist Wilder Penfield, whose research tends to affirm the powerful role played by memory in the scenario of life.

Dr. Penfield, the late Canadian neurosurgeon, devised a technique whereby he could activate various parts of the conscious, living brain. He found that stimulation over the temporal lobe by means of a weak electric current sometimes plunged his patients back in time. In a book titled *The Cerebral Cortex of Man,* he wrote, "A young man . . . cried out when his right temporal lobe was being stimulated: 'Yes doctor! Yes, doctor! Now I hear laughing — my friends — in South Africa!' It seemed to him," continued Dr. Penfield, "that he was with his cousins at home . . . he and the two ladies were laughing. The scene was as clear to him as if he had recalled the event from memory thirty seconds after it happened. Sight and sound and personal interpretation were all recreated by the stimulation of the electrode." Penfield named the phenomenon *flashback* — a process whereby the brain replays a tape of a previous experience, like TV instant replay.

"When, by chance, the neurosurgeon's electrode activates past experience," related the doctor, "that experience unfolds progressively . . . like a tape recording or a strip of cinematographic film. As long as the electrode is held in place, the experience of a former day goes forward. There is no holding it still, no turning back. When the electrode is withdrawn, it stops as suddenly as it began."

People facing imminent death — from drowning or falling, for example — see their life memory tapes flash before their eyes in an instant. What inferences can we draw from these remarkable flashback phenomena? "Consciousness, forever flowing past . . . is recorded. The recording, made up of passing potentials in the everchanging circuits within the brain, is astonishingly complete. . . ." The thread of time remains with us in the form of electrical transcriptions, tape recordings in the memory bank of your hundred-billion-cell biocomputer, your brain. This thread travels through the nerve cells and across the synapses, the junctions between them. As Dr. Penfield put it, "On the thread of time are strung, like pearls in unending succession, patterns that can still recall the vanished content of a former awareness." Neurophysiologist Dr. Karl Pribram cautions, "Penfield's results cannot be obtained from the normal human brain. There must be a scar which does the organizing of the stimulus pattern, making it look as if a tape were present." With this reservation in mind, let's pursue Penfield's image.

How far back does it stretch, this thread of time? Sigmund Freud and Arthur Janov have theorized that it stretches back to the womb.

Freud introduced the concept of *birth trauma*. According to this widely accepted theory, suffering inflicted on the baby during the birth process is reflected as inappropriate behavior (neurosis) in the adult. Dr. Janov, director of the Primal Institute of Los Angeles, built on Penfield's theory when he devised a method to induce primal scream: an experience not unlike Dr. Penfield's flashback phenomenon. Dr. Janov's method is said to activate the neural circuitry, to release the tape which replays the patient's birth experience. Like Penfield's patients, Janov's subjects are plunged backwards in time to relive a dimly remebered past.

Like life events, our beliefs, opinions, and shoulds — everything we've ever been taught or warned against — are securely stored in complete detail on memory tapes inside the brain. They are accessible to the mind (although not always to the conscious mind) in a wink of our magnificent biocomputer's complex circuitry. Thus, for example, the sight of a red dress on a total stranger may trigger a sudden burst of irrational fear and nausea by subconscious association with some long forgotten event locked in memory. Stroking a friendly cat may bring on the familiar sneezes of hay fever or the itchy symptoms of hives. Memories interweave with our daily experiences in countless subtle ways, influencing thought, perception, emotion, and behavior. Is it possible that memory tapes of past illnesses are triggered into instant replay when we find ourselves in circumstances similar to those that triggered the initial symptoms? Or, is it possible that memory sometimes interferes with our ability to turn on the natural immune system?

Perhaps the natural function of memory is to allow us to *avoid* repetition of past experiences that might hinder our evolution. Certainly one obvious purpose of memory is to teach us not to burn our hands twice on a hot stove. We may, however, burn our hands senselessly and repeatedly until we get the psyche's message. Some people get sick senselessly and repeatedly. What's the message for them?

Before we look at possible answers to this crucial question, let's consider another problem which is related: Are you operating the tape recorder—or is it operating you? Driven by the instinct to survive, the human mind, our tape recorder, behaves like a virus. Perceiving the world of things, that which exists, mind projects our perceptions through the distorting lens of tapes and belief structures. This compels us to organize and 'conquer' our surroundings, to convert that which *is* into that which *should be*. A virus senses the normal metabolic activity of the host cell (that which is) and reprograms it. Instead of producing protoplasm, the mysterious elixir of life, the cell exhausts its precious protein supply making more virus (that which should be). A virus, like a gene, is naked DNA. A cell is a factory which converts formless energy into living matter. The gene is the template.

A template is essentially a piece of information—a bit of memory. Like a punchcard in a computer, it mobilizes and directs operations to reproduce a certain form (virus cell, or situation) from data contained in the memory bank (gene, virus, or previous experience). In the case of the virus or the gene, the instructions are encoded in the form of various arrangements of protein molecules on nucleic acid chains. In the case of mind, the template consists of a patterned arrangement of electrochemical potentials (a belief) in the neural structure of the brain, potentials that may be activated by incoming perceptual data. Beliefs, drawn from the dead past, are used as templates by the mind to shape present experience in the form of past events we feel we can control. Thus the mind constantly attempts to achieve power over the present by reimposing carefully selected portions of the past on its environment. The desire for power, based on the instinctive urge to survive, is an ancient mind tape. It's the mental equivalent of the body's reproductive urge.

Rational mind, we have suggested, is a creature of memory. Its concerns are the fixed, musty rememberings of the dead past. Its archenemy is emotion — raw, irrational, surging, here-and-now emotion. Variations on a single theme, emotions like lust, hate, and anxiety are three faces of a single energy. We might call it the energy of arousal, the urge to live and grow, the energy of expansion, the stirrings of spring. Rational mind tries to control this energy just as it tries to control its environment, by forcing it to conform to belief templates. But the energy of arousal and growth refuses to be compartmentalized, confined, and controlled; conflict results.

Let's consider a specific example. Perhaps on a particular morning, you awaken with a feeling of sexual desire. Your first perception of the day may have been a tune orchestrated by body hormones, arousal by the warm body of a sleeping mate. The refrain is as old as the phenomenon of life itself.

Delicately modulating levels of sex hormones and adrenaline in the bloodstream, physical being beguiles the attention of awakening awareness. "I want," says the body in the feeling language of the hormonal system. Scanning its memory bank in response to the nonverbal body stimulus, rational mind flashes back a thought. "Control yourself. You have to get up and go to work."

"I want!" body repeats more imperiously, perhaps punctuating its demand with a slight secretion from the appropriate organ and reaching a hand to touch the body next to it. The mate awakens, yawns, and declines to participate. Rapidly reviewing its recipes, mind considers its response. "Well, sex is bad for you," it may reply, or maybe it prints out a pattern of thoughts which goes something like, "If you were really spiritual, you'd rise above and transcend your baser animal urges." (Recall that body and mind are not separate from one another or from their surroundings — the conflict arises from different tapes in the same biocomputer.)

The battle of the tapes, between the emotional body tape and the rational mind tape, is on! Seizing control of the endocrine system by means of nerve-hormone interactions between the thinking brain and the pituitary, the master endocrine gland, anger alters the delicate balance of blood-borne hormones. The mate may be the unwitting and surprised recipient of some cutting remark at this point.

Love, the primal energy of life, reverses polarity, manifesting its opposite face: rage. Adrenaline provides the energy, *mind determines the direction*. As in the case of virulent infection, the victim feels attacked, invaded, and overcome — as if possessed by a demon. The red-eyed monster is indeed a demon, an ancient tape programming the body through the endocrine system — programming it to fight. Carl Jung tells us that a primal, ancient argument has been going on between male and female. This battle has been waged in every human language, in every part of the globe, since the beginning of human existence.

Have you ever been jealous? Can you remember how your body felt? Did you suffer? Think about the power of jealousy, a pure mind trip. Like absurdly warped funhouse mirrors, mind tapes reflect distorted views of us and our experiences, shaping our realities. Change the tapes, and you change your experience of that reality.

7 / The Mystical Marriage

YIN		YANG
Female		*Male*
Passive		*Active*
Moon		*Sun*
Earth		*Heaven*

IN AN IMPORTANT SENSE, then, life is a mystical marriage. It is mystical because it seems to embrace incompatible opposites like male and female, love and hate, birth and death, success and failure, sickness and health. Often we may seem to ourselves to be not one personality, but two — living different aspects of the same life. Have you ever said to yourself, "I don't want to feel like this"? That's an interesting statement, because it assumes that the person who has the 'want' has no influence over the person who is feeling 'like this'. Yet they are both you. I sometimes get that double message from patients who come into my office. One part of them wants to be sick, another parts wants to be well, and the party of the first part, the sick body, has the upper hand at the time.

Who is it that brings a set of symptoms into the medical clinic, doctor's office, or hospital? What do we know about this hypothetical patient? Is there any scientific basis for assuming some kind of double configuration in the way the patient experiences himself or herself?

Split-brain researchers state that the two halves of the brain (the left and right cerebral hemispheres) correspond to two potentially independent minds. The left-brain hemisphere is said to operate in the logical, sequential and verbal modes. The right-brain hemisphere is dubbed visual, timeless, and intuitive. Traditionally, the logical mode has been associated more with maleness, while the intuitive mode is more frequently associated with femaleness.

Theories about hemispheric specialization are not universally accepted. Once again Dr. Pribram urges caution: "Females are consistently superior in all linguistic activities which are left hemisphere. They may also be more intuitive and therefore more right hemispheric. This leaves us males with no hemispheres. Any explanation of hemispheric function in organizing our civilization must take all of the evidence into account, and this evidence at the moment doesn't fit together in any simplistic fashion."

In my case records, I describe a patient as 'male' or 'female' — a common and traditional distinction in medical case histories, but one which is not exactly true. In the developing foetus are two sets of ducts. One set makes male sex organs, the other makes female sex organs. A decision is made by a throw of the genes, and one set develops as the other atrophies, but not completely. Scientific research has found that certain hormones are associated with the development and maintenance of female sex characteristics and others with the development of male sex characteristics. Although these have been conveniently labeled as 'male sex hormones' and 'female sex hormones', we find that both sexes secrete detectable amounts of each kind. It isn't the presence of one set of hormones and the absence of the other that determines masculinity or femininity, but the quantitative preponderance of one set of hormones over the other.

It is possible for our hypothetical patient to be a husky

deep-voiced woman with a primarily rational, sequential mental orientation — but a 'normal' woman nevertheless. It is equally possible for our patient to be a slender, mild-mannered man with an evidently intuitional mental set — who may also be happily married and raising a family. The combination of left- or right-brain orientation with the male or female hormonal balance results in a broad spectrum of masculine and feminine characteristics among those who are distinctly male or female in terms' of the primary sex characteristics delivered to them by a throw of the genes. In recent years it's become evident that not everyone is willing to accept physical sex characteristics as a one-way ticket to a particular sexual identity.

Some men state flatly that they are females trapped in male bodies. Of these, a few have undergone cosmetic surgical procedures, and after an artificial adjustment in the balance of sex hormones, presto! they've become transformed into sexually functioning females. It is not unreasonable to point out that every man contains within him a living, active, and potentially dominant female aspect. The same is true in reverse for women. Those men and women who vigorously object to social and sexual roles being forced upon them simply because of inherited physical sex characteristics offer an important and potentially useful clue for understanding health and dis-ease from still another perspective.

As previously mentioned, people are like snowflakes — no two of us are alike. The mystical marriage of mind and body, of male and female aspects in each of us may provide a unique formula or pattern that is intimately connected to our unfolding evolution as individuals. Violate the pattern, repress some portion of the formula, and you become a patient in the doctor's waiting room.

A man unable to express tenderness because it violates his image of masculinity, a woman unwilling to accept a challenging executive position because it conflicts with her image of feminity—both are facing situations in which internalized distress may lead to illness. In such situations, the masculine side is at war with the feminine side, with the body as the battleground. But in most cases, the rivalry between male and female modes of consciousness is more subtle.

The manner in which the symptom is presented by the patient—the cough, joint pain, bellyache, anxiety, or depression—can be used to get a handle on the issues involved in the conflict. A symptom is a form of energy. When I ask someone to describe their ache or pain, I'm asking them to transform that energy into a particular mental image.

Let's look at some examples. Suppose a patient consults me about a backache. In the course of our preliminary conversation I ask, "What brings you here today?" People operating in the masculine left-brain mode often respond to this query with a verbal diagnosis. "I have arthritis," they might reply. Those oriented toward the feminine right-brain side of their being use descriptions that convey feeling and direct experience such as "I'm in pain" or "My back went out." My next question, "What does it feel like?" is specifically designed to shift attention from the word-making left brain to the picture-making right brain.

When attention is shifted from thoughts to sensations, the feminine mode of knowing is invoked. The instruction to make a simple picture of how it feels is a command to the right cerebral hemisphere to project a hologram, a three-dimensional image, into the mind's eye. "It feels like there's a knife stuck in my back." "My lower spine is tied in a knot." "I feel like a cement block is jammed into my body." These are samples of holograms experienced and described by patients under treatment. The exact border of the pain, the junction with parts of the body that feel normal and healthy, often has a three-dimensional shape that can be precisely described and measured. That, according to science, makes it real.

Outlining the borders of her seven-year-old chronic backache, a patient said, "It feels like there's a snake wrapped around my backbone." The snake was about seven inches long and one-half inch thick, according to her description. Treatment involved asking her to concentrate on her breathing, to imagine energy circulating up the front of her body and down the back, then to count off a short sequence of numbers. When the counting stopped, she visualized herself in a beautiful place. In this manner she was able to turn off her thinker, her masculine left hemisphere. She then commanded her right hemisphere to create a visual image of the snake moving down her spine, out of her body, and into the ocean. As she watched this spectacle with her mind's eye, she simultaneously felt it happening in her body. "The pain is gone!" she announced in amazement as the snake slithered into the sea. Shifting from left-brain rational thought to a right-brain visual image succeeded in alleviating her physical symptoms.

Similarly, a man with a herniated disk pictured a pair of pliers coming out of his back and dropping into the ocean. Another patient found that his migraine headache disappeared when he pictured the dissolution of an imaginary ice pick in his head. The shift from the rational mode of thinking to the visual mode can sometimes accomplish wonders in dealing with painful symptoms.

The procedures previously described are not offered as substitutes for effective emergency care. In case of heart attack, serious accidents, or sudden onset of violent illness, emergency room and intensive care procedures are the treatment of choice. A sense of intense pressure may accompany heart attack, and it may feel like an elephant is sitting on one's chest. Negotiating with the elephant and picturing it getting off can be tried as an adjunct to standard coronary care — unless none is available. Then one is in the position of the snakebite victim with the snakestone, isn't one?

How can a picture in your mind affect a real pain in your body? Remember what Carl Jung said about some people thinking of the psyche as a closed system? Assuming the psyche to be one with the body, many patients are not surprised at this demonstrable power of their own minds. Mostly they are delighted that the symptoms abate. Is it possible that the physician can help affect the course of disease by altering the patient's view of that disease? Is what my patients think they have, how they view their plight, as important as the X-ray picture or the computer printout from the pathology laboratory? Can an alteration in the psyche produce a corresponding change in the real, physical matter of the body? Make a fist and see for yourself. Your hand moves in space-time at your command.

It seems like a kind of miracle, doesn't it? — to make a picture in your mind and have a seven-year-old pain disappear. It is, and so is the ability of penicillin to restore a pneumonia or scarlet fever patient to health. I can remember infusing metycaine and cortisone into painful shoulder joints. In cases of subdeltoid bursitis, a severely incapacitating and very painful shoulder condition, the concoction stopped the pain within minutes. I thought that was a miracle. I still do.

The data from my own clinical experiments and reports from people like Drs. Carl Jung, C. Norman Shealy, David Bressler of UCLA's pain clinic, and a host of others suggest that your control over the function and malfunction of your body may be greater than you think. With practice it may become complete and absolute. It's possible that your body will do anything you want it to do. It's possible that everything your body does is something you've told it to do.

"Hold on now!" you may say. "Are you trying to tell us that people create their own illnesses? One would have to be crazy to purposely make oneself sick." That's true, I agree. But suppose you're not one, but two — as previously suggested. One side of you wants to be sick, while the other wants to get well. One part of you creates and actively maintains the illness. The complementary opposite side sincerely and honestly wants to be rid of it. It is the responsibility and the task of the physician to help shift the balance from one side to the other. Let's look at a possible scenario.

The male side deals with space-time concerns like making a living, maintaining a reputation, achieving goals, and getting things done. In our rational Western culture, we may associate the male side with 'mind' as the weaver and keeper of our beliefs, opinions, and shoulds. The feminine side, with its feeling, visualizing, and intuitional modes, is responsible for the body. Mind, the male, may be setting a pace which is a bit too fast for his mate, the body. Our plans, schedules, and activities may be pushing our body's tolerance toward its limit. "I really wish you wouldn't do that," is her usual response. Since she doesn't care much for language, she communicates this through feelings. You might feel tired all the time. Your joints might ache, or perhaps you just feel grumpy and out of sorts. If you ignore her, if you persist in your ways in spite of clear indications from your body that she doesn't like it, your symptoms get worse. Perhaps you begin to experience runny nose and other symptoms of a cold or the flu.

At this point many follow the advice of the TV commercials. They take cold tablets or some other over-the-counter drug which promises to mask the symptoms while the happy user relentlessly drives the complaining body in the service of chattering mind. Witness the TV commercial messages which depict people with all the symptoms of pneumonia and influenza swallowing pills and then driving taxicabs, dancing at parties, and shoveling show. This is the final insult. Body says, "That's it! I don't want to play any more. I quit." The patient experiences complete collapse.

A better way would be to resolve the conflict in its early stages. We would have to pay closer attention to communications from the body in response to our current mind trips or ego trips — and take those communications seriously. We would have to realize that the dominance of the left-brain hemisphere (rational, linear, male side) or of the right-brain hemisphere (intuitional, nonlinear, female side) in our experience doesn't mean that we can safely neglect or ignore the nondominant side. We can assume that a certain balance between the two is necessary to achieve and maintain a state of health and well-being. There's no formula for a correct balance because no two of us are alike — so you can relax and write your own prescription.

Like the hypothetical rings around the psyche, the apparent conflict between mind and body, male and female, left and right cerebral hemispheres is illusory. The illusion of conflict becomes real only as we identify with it, believe in it, and become attached to it. The natural state is one of harmony between these illusorily battling opposites, and by giving up our extramarital affair with illusion, we can let the mystical marriage work according to its natural loving design.

PART III

Psychosomatics: The Evidence

"The stuff of the world is mind-stuff."
— SIR ARTHUR EDDINGTON (1882–1944)

8 / Stress and Distress

*"Your pain is the breaking of the shell that
encloses your understanding."*
— KAHLIL GIBRAN (1883–1931)
The Prophet

PREVIOUSLY, we introduced the notion that the human factor, the psyche, plays a vital role in turning on the placebo
effect or the body's natural immune system. We have also
suggested that the latter two processes may be the same,
that the placebo effect may simply result from the psyche
activating the natural immune system. Beliefs, opinions,
and shoulds, we have theorized, may seriously affect our
health and well-being, particularly when we abstract our
innermost selves from our bodies and view the matter of
our bodies and the universe around us as lifeless, particulate matter. Eliminating the illusory borders between mind,
body, and environment, we discover that we are dealing
with a single interconnected system, a continuum.

In this and the immediately following chapters, I would
like to present some of the evidence supporting that view.
The evidence we shall consider was presented at a symposium titled "On the Nature and Management of Stress,"
co-sponsored by the Extension Division of the University of
California at Santa Cruz and UCLA, and co-moderated by
Dr. David Bressler, director of the UCLA Pain Clinic, and

myself. At this symposium eminent researchers from the disciplines of medicine, psychology, and philosophy shared the fruits of their lives' work.

The term *psychosomatic* made its first appearance near the beginning of the nineteenth century, but it was not until the early part of this century that medical researchers began to accept the notion that physical disease could involve a mental component. Today, it's fair to say that most health professionals comfortably view ailments like asthma, colitis, and allergies as having mental or emotional components. But more recent research suggests that a far greater range of pathologic processes may be classified as psychosomatic.

When Dr. Hans Selye of Montreal introduced the concept of *stress* into the medical literature, he performed a shotgun marriage between Doctor Medicine and Madame Psychology. He joined the two when he presented evidence that *disease and distress can flow from our psychological attitudes toward environmental events.*

Chatting before a thousand people at our stress symposium in Monterey, California, Dr. Selye shared accomplishments and insights gleaned from a life in its eighth decade. Like Einstein, he believes that his momentous discoveries did not emerge from his rational mind. "All great discoveries," he said, "have one big requirement. In order to make a great discovery, you must begin with a great dream."

Dr. Selye, recalling his days as a medical student at the University of Prague, described the insight that led him from the atomistic view to the holistic perspective of medical practice. Examining a child from the pediatric service of the university hospital, his professor looked into the child's mouth, discovered little white spots called *Koplick's spots,* and made his diagnosis: measles. That announcement made a tremendous impression on the nineteen-year-old medical student. Measles, he thought, is caused by a life form so small it can't be seen under the microscope. Yet the teacher could identify it merely by looking into the child's mouth. The young student then had an afterthought which changed his whole career.

"It's curious," he thought to himself, "that all patients, whether they have cancer of the liver, measles, indigestion, or gastrointestinal disease, have something in common. They look sick. Their faces all show that they don't feel well. They don't want to get up, they feel weak, they have no appetite. It doesn't matter what their disease is." He wondered why no one had ever studied the syndrome of just being sick. If you could cure that syndrome, Selye reasoned, it wouldn't matter what caused it.

When he shared this idea with his professor of physiology, Selye recalls, "he laughed in my face, saying that it was such a silly idea that even if I provided my own money, time, and materials, he wouldn't permit research like that to go on in his university." Conventional medical wisdom at that time held, and still insists, that illness, in general, must be treated by finding a specific cause and applying the specific cure.

It seems obvious that you can't cure mercury poisoning by giving polio vaccine. All of medicine is based on the concept of *specificity*. You have to find out what's wrong with your patient before you can give the proper treatment. Nineteen years old, and ignorant of this basic tenet of medical orthodoxy, young Selye continued to ponder his concept of treating the syndrome of just being sick. That was back in 1926. "Since everyone laughed at me, I thought the idea must be stupid, and I forgot about it for a while," Dr. Selye recalled.

The idea surfaced years later when Selye was professor of biochemistry at McGill University in Canada. Injecting impure ovarian tissue extract into test animals, he found that the procedure produced a characteristic syndrome, or set of symptoms. All treated animals showed decrease in the size of the thymus gland and lymph nodes, along with enlargement and increased activity of the adrenal glands. A third finding, induced by the impurities in the injected material, was the appearance of ulcers in the stomach of the treated animal. Dr. Selye named this symptom triad the *stress syndrome* or the *alarm reaction.* "That was mainly due," he says, "to my ignorance of the English language. I didn't know the difference between the concepts of 'stress' and 'strain.'" The social, psychological, or physical force is the stress; the syndrome of being sick is the strain. In physics and engineering, strain represents resistance of a system to an outside force of change (stress). In Selye's model, distress, or being sick, is a function of *resistance* to the stressor, the force of change in the environment.

Ten years after its first stirrings as an afterthought in the mind of the nineteen-year-old medical student, a description of the classical symptoms of just being sick appeared in the British journal, *Nature.* In that publication, Selye coined the phrase *general adaptation syndrome,* which describes the way in which the body defends itself against environmental change. That description has since become a classic in the medical literature all over the world. He showed that the changes seen in the alarm reaction occur in response to many different agents. The axiom that *all* sickness arises from a specific cause was shattered.

In humans we encounter another factor — social interaction. In order for a social event to produce bodily changes there has to be some intermediary process. This intermediary process, the thinking mind, interprets the social event as threatening or stressful. Someone may say, "I don't love you any more." A spouse may insist, "I want a divorce." You may notice that you can't find your wallet or purse. Emotional thoughts about such events can precipitate physical distress and disease. If you don't think about it, you don't experience distress.

A sudden increase in temperature or decrease in the oxygen content of the environment doesn't require an intellectual interpretation in order for the body to react, but events in the social environment do. Social events are not *in themselves* capable of raising blood pressure, or instigating sweaty palms, headaches, or heart attacks. But the thoughts that follow them often induce worry, anxiety, and nervous tension, perhaps later followed by more serious consequences.

Thoughts, of course, can't arise from a vacuum, but emerge through a filter of beliefs, opinions, and shoulds in the mind of the thinker. Worried, anxious thoughts that accompany certain social, financial, and psychological situations have the capacity, it seems, to inflict damage upon the body and its organs. Philosopher J. Krishnamurti compares the intellectual thought process to a rattlesnake. We exercise caution in regard to rattlesnakes because we are well aware of their dangerous potential. Krishnamurti suggests that we be equally wary regarding our thought-making mind, the wellspring of beliefs, opinions, and shoulds.

Stress as defined by scientists and engineers is an external force applied to a system. Distress may represent *the resistance of the thinking mind to change*. Persistent resistance and constant struggle can be harmful and even lethal to the physical organism. Goings on in the social environment can't make us sick. Worrying about them does.

People who worry experience the strain of anxiety as a consequence of stress. They are more prone than those who don't to a host of ailments. Perhaps worry makes us sick because the mind activates the body's defenses in a struggle against change. Perhaps sickness is a signal from the psyche telling us to let go and flow with the change. It seems that certain attitudes toward life set off the body's alarm reaction needlessly. The alarm is sounded by the intellect.

Elaborating on his view of stress as a nonspecific disease-causing agent, Dr. Selye compares it with the concept of energy. Energy is a very general concept. You can derive it from a waterfall, burning petroleum or coal, or from nuclear fission. A tankful of gasoline, a stick of dynamite, and a lump of uranium are all forms of energy, a nonspecific carrier of power which can light a lamp, lift an airliner, grow a geranium, or destroy a city. Stress, according to the man who invented the medical concept, is a form of energy. *Stress is force acting on form.* Marital disagreement, job frustration, combat fatigue, or skin burns may all produce the same bodily changes. What, we may ask, does marital disagreement have to do with skin burns? How can they both gnaw holes in someone's stomach? Like steam and electricity, each is a specific example of a nonspecific, broader concept: *energy* in one case, and *stress* in the other.

Let's follow Selye's elaboration of his concept. "The source of stress is specific (a stressor). The results of stress are specific (diseases). Stress itself, like energy, is nonspecific. When different agents act as stressors, they may induce peptic ulcers, psychiatric disorders, heart attacks, strokes, or high blood pressure, depending on one's personal disposition. The weakest link in the body breaks under stress. Hormone blood level changes, and other measurable body reactions caused by suffering, by grief, or by great joy, are exactly the same. Stress is the nonspecific response of the body to any demand made upon it — any demand, good or bad. *If you have to adapt, you are under stress.*

A keystone in our emerging mosaic is the research on the pathway by which a scary thought becomes a rapid heart rate. The work done by Dr. Roger Guillemin and associates at the Salk Institute in California won a Nobel Prize for isolating chemical substances from the base of the brain which transmit messages from the thinking brain to the pituitary—the master gland of the endocrine system. Evanescent thoughts, electrochemical nerve impulses, stimulate the flow of hormones, the chemical compounds which vitally affect and control the function of every cell in your body. The substances which connect the psychological with the physical are called *neurohumoral transducers*. They receive electrical nerve impulses from the brain and transform them into chemical messengers which travel through the bloodstream. The chemical compound precisely replicates the message carried by the electrical thought.

According to Selye, peaceful thoughts release peaceful hormones, just as aggressive and fearful thoughts release aggressive and fearful hormones. "Hormones have been isolated, and nonhormone substances have been synthesized which have either *syntoxic* or *catatoxic* effects." Syntoxic hormones are dubbed "hormones of harmonious cooperation" by Dr. Selye. "They are the doves among the hormones. Cortisone is one of those. They are the tissue tranquilizers." They tell the tissue to relax, the issue isn't worth an alarm reaction. Their complementary opposites, the catatoxic hormones, are the hormones of aggression and of resistance. Adrenalin, which mediates the fight-or-flight reaction, is an example. Dr. Selye suggests that there are also syntoxic and catatoxic attitudes.

Hans Selye had a chance to test his theories in his own life when he found out that he had cancer. "I never thought I could cure it myself. That isn't what I wanted to do. I was convinced that I would be dead in one year." Dr. Selye adopted a syntoxic attitude toward his potentially fatal disease. "I just decided that in a year I could accomplish a lot, so why not use it?" Throwing himself into his work, he ignored the malignant process in his body. "I had a little bit of luck," he recalls. The tumor disappeared spontaneously.

Dr. Selye shared his experience with oncologists (cancer specialists) at an international symposium on stress, death, and cancer, co-sponsored by New York's Sloan-Kettering Cancer Institute and his own International Institute of Stress. "[Scientists at the symposium] strongly believed that through the stress I placed on my immunologic system, I probably played a great role in curing my own cancer." Like Coley's Toxins, or any other stressor, hard work had stimulated the body's immune system to rouse itself and destroy the tumor.

Set this hard scientific opinion beside the theory of Krahenbuhl and Remington who stated, "If we can discover how to activate the immune system, we may have a successful way to fight cancer." Hans Selye, doctor of medicine, doctor of science, points to a way when he says, "The will to live is a great curative force." To date, Dr. Selye's Institute of Stress has collected over a hundred well-documented scientific articles concerning the curative effects of patient attitudes in cancer cases. He will not at this time claim that he cured his own cancer by his attitude, yet he considers the subject far from closed. "My cancer *was* cured, and I have that attitude," he says with a grin.

Dr. Hans Selye has won worldwide acclaim and recognition for his fundamental contribution to our understand-of the way in which mental strain can change the body. Like Albert Einstein, Hans Selye fused a pair of opposite, incompatible concepts, sparking a quantum leap in human consciousness. Einstein fused energy and matter, showing them to be functions of light. Selye wed mind with body, showing both to be functions of consciousness. While psychologists and medical doctors were arguing about which was primary — mind or body, psyche or soma, consciousness or brain — his meticulous research produced hard scientific evidence that the two are one.

That the intellect can initiate real physical disease is a revolutionary idea. Society's conventional wisdom teaches that if something is all in your mind, it doesn't really matter.

It doesn't matter because it isn't *real*. An event isn't real, I was taught, if no one outside my mind experiences it. Only I experience my thoughts. Having no space-time dimensions, my thoughts can't be measured, verified, or validated by anyone else. If they aren't real, they can't hurt me, I've been told. Yet there is evidence now to the contrary.

"Our usual codes of behavior," Dr. Selye relates, "always tell us something about how to live, how to be happy and healthy, how to enjoy life. These prescriptions usually begin with admonitions like 'Thou shalt' or 'Thou shalt not'. Most codes are based on some infallible authority which you have to follow... a god, a political leader, a philosopher. They all prescribe." Concerning his concept of stress, Dr. Selye adds, "In this area, I do not prescribe.... I do not tell you what to do. I collect the stones and polish them nicely for you, but you are the mosaic maker."

9 / Taking It to Heart

*"Be observant if you would have a pure heart,
for something is born to you in consequence of
every action."*

— JALALUDDIN RUMI (1207–1273)

DR. HANS SELYE'S work has brilliantly delineated a holistic model of the means by which we humans can think ourselves sick. One implication of this model is that the actual appearance of disease is preceded by a response to stress dictated by the respondent's belief system, his or her code of life. At this point, it would be useless for a doctor to attempt to diagnose or prescribe, since the problem is rooted in attitudes, not organs. Each of us selects and places the stones that make up our individual life mosaics, and the resulting work of art is so complex that only the artist dares tamper with it. "You are the mosaic maker," says Dr. Selye. "You must be your own doctor."

Simple logic tells us that certain attitudes may be characterized by recognizable behavior patterns. How do people respond to stress in terms of behavior?

Dr. Meyer Friedman, head of the cardiology department of San Francisco's Mount Zion Hospital has carried out important research on the relationship between attitudes, behavior, and heart attack. Dr. Friedman's data and conclusions outlined at the University of California stress seminar are consistent with the model proposed by Dr. Selye. In his book *Type A Behavior and Your Heart,* Dr. Friedman examines the response of people to stress at the level of action.

A certain type of behavior, according to Friedman's work, precipitates the experience of coronary occlusion (heart attack). He calls this *Type A behavior.* People who have heart attacks seem to be individuals who are "engaged in a continuous here and now struggle against time, other people, or both, always accompanied by an emotional overlay of frustration, hostility, or both." The attitude which patterns and precipitates this type of behavior can evolve out of a disturbed perception of normal social factors, or from a correct perception of disturbed social factors. Dr. Friedman observes that, "Our society may be so disturbed that anyone with accurate perceptions of it might well have emotional reactions." Type As look out at the world and see a preponderance of injustice, evil, and danger. They believe that this malevolent reality is material, physical, and separated from the psyche, cut off by a border of skin enclosing the physical body. They see survival as the result of a successful struggle against a hostile environment — the real world.

"These people," says cardiologist Friedman, "think that achievement guarantees status." The more achievement, the higher the status, the surer the survival. The struggle for more and more achievement, when accompanied by frustration and hostility, precipitates the heart attack. Observing their experience, Type As construct a mental pattern, a belief structure in which they see themselves as alone and isolated in a dog-eat-dog world whose motto is, "Every man for himself and devil take the hindmost."

Clawing upward toward status and survival, Type As may jettison considerations like personal growth, cultural stimulation, spiritual experience, affection, and love. There is simply no space or time for these frivolities in the Type A lifestyle. "When we come to the coronary patient, we have a person who is essentially bankrupt in these areas," observed Dr. Friedman. One might even say that they die of a broken heart.

"After a first heart attack," he continued, "there is no effective method for preventing a second attack as medicine is now practiced. No cardiologist using current therapy can prevent a second heart attack in a patient. Lowering blood pressure doesn't help, lowering blood cholesterol doesn't help, and, in my opinion, physical exercise is probably killing more coronary patients than it is helping.... At the expense of forty million dollars, the federal government has just completed a study which concludes that in patients with coronary disease who have been given drugs to lower blood cholesterol, the mortality rate is exactly the same as the mortality rate among patients who have had no such drugs."

There is a twenty-year-old ongoing study of the causative factors in heart disease, called *The Framingham Study*. Thousands of citizens of the town of Framingham, Massachusetts, have been under observation over the past two decades to determine the relationship of environmental factors to the incidence of heart disease. Sponsored by the U.S. Public Health Service at a cost of over fifty million dollars, The Framingham Study has recently examined the role played by anger and frustration. Researchers have reported, on an eight-year follow-up of 1,670 normal individuals, that males who were Type A developed chest pains three times as often as did their peaceful and placid Type B neighbors. Type A women reporting the onset of pain in the chest over the eight-year observation period outnumbered their more serene Type B sisters by a ratio of four to one. Type A citizens developed organic heart disease twice as often as Type B people.

Where does this leave our currently popular theories? What about the role of overeating or cigarette smoking? Doesn't high blood pressure and high cholesterol predispose one to heart attack? The Framingham Study showed that people who are peaceful and calm rather than competitive and uptight rarely show elevations of blood cholesterol, *no matter what they eat!* Cardiologist Friedman emphasizes the key role played by a syntoxic (placid) attitude toward life. "If a real Type B-4 person [the most relaxed] ever has a heart attack and dies, we'll pay for the funeral." He hasn't seen that happen once in seventeen years of scientific testing of his hypothesis.

Our attempts to eliminate heart disease by eradicating high blood pressure, high serum cholesterol, and smoking are like trying to destroy a tree by cutting off its branches. These signs and symptoms *accompany* heart disease, they do not *cause* it. They're the Koplick's spots of heart disease. If you find little white Koplick's spots in someone's mouth, you can, like Selye's pediatrics professor, consistently predict a measles attack. You can predict it, but you can do nothing to prevent it. If we treated measles the way we treat heart disease, we would spend hundreds of millions of dollars trying to develop drugs and surgical procedures to eliminate Koplick's spots.

Suppose we combine the reports of Selye and Friedman. Perhaps the mosaic we make of these stones will disclose a more rational solution to the problem of heart disease. Picture a tree. The fruit of our tree is heart disease. Among the branches bearing that bitter fruit are high blood pressure, high blood cholesterol, heavy smoking, overeating, and lack of physical exercise. Branches are specialized forms of the trunk. If you chop down the trunk, you destroy the branches so they can produce no more heart attacks. Let's use Selye's term *stress response* to describe the trunk which bears the branches and the fruit of heart disease. It is the

stress of constant, moment-to-moment anger and frustration which branches into smoking, eating, and hypertension,
and finally produces heart attack, the fruit of frustrated
anger. At the root of our tree of death, we find an attitude,
a way of thinking.

The root cause of heart attack, disease, and suffering
has many names. Dr. Meyer Friedman calls it *Type A attitude,* Hans Selye dubbed it the *catatoxic attitude,* Roberto
Assagioli spoke of *identification,* and Gautama Buddha
used the term *attachment.* At the root of stress, mother of
heart attack, disease, and human suffering, lies a thought
pattern, a way of being. According to UCLA's Dr. Barbara
Brown, human distress is "essentially and exclusively a
consequence of intellectual activity."

Starting at the root, the tree grows as follows: First
the victim decides that survival depends on status enhancement. That to them is the most important thing in life. This
radical decision is linked with the equally radical notion
that perpetual achievement is the only path to enhanced
status. Intellectual activity spawns space-time activity which
manifests a perpetual battle against deadlines and competitors. During the constant, minute-to-minute struggle, the
victim feels rage and frustration in relation to obstacles in
the way of achievement and status enhancement. In the
never ending war against competitors and obstacles, he or
she ignores, neglects, and loses the stabilizing influence of
vital forces — affection, love, spiritual growth, and cultural
stimulation. Deprived of these life-giving energies, the victim turns to substitutes. Some overeat, some smoke a great
deal, while others turn to loveless sex. Combinations of the
above habits are frequent. All are branches of the rapidly
growing trunk-like mass of rage and frustration, the rising
tide of trapped emotional energy.

As the trunk of emotional energy gets bigger and more
obvious, it becomes visible — people notice that the victim

is under stress. Soon, fed by the dual roots of belief structure and constant struggle, the mushrooming psychological
mass invades the physical body. The patient suffers, experiences distress, and develops physical symptoms. The examining physician may discover hypertension and/or hyper-
cholesterolemia as evidence of the invasion. While physician,
patient, and druggist hack frantically at these branches,
the victim's nagging notion that you have to struggle to
survive proceeds inexorably to fruition. He or she develops
a heart attack and dies, forfeiting the very survival which
was the purpose of the fearful struggle. One wonders if this
kind of behavior is what Shakespeare had in mind when
he wrote the line, "What fools these mortals be!"

If we accept Charles Darwin's theory of the survival
of the fittest, we might see heart disease as nature's way of
phasing out unfit forms of behavior—aggression, greed,
status seeking, and other catatoxic activity patterns.

What are the possible mechanisms by which disturbed
thinking and emotional imbalance become heart disease?
Selye thinks that it's an excess of catatoxic hormones reflecting an unbalanced mental attitude, a catastrophe-oriented
thought process. Friedman's data supports Selye's hypothesis. He has found that, in the course of an ordinary day,
Type A people secrete almost twice as much norepinephrine (a catatoxic, adrenaline-like substance) as do placid or
Type B people. During non-working hours and during sleep,
secretion levels are the same for both groups. Adrenaline,
alias epinephrine, is released into the blood by the adrenal
gland whose name it bears. Norepinephrine, a close relative
of adrenaline, is made and stored in the sympathetic nerve
endings; when released, it affects all the vital organs—heart,
arteries, stomach, and so forth. While parasympathetic nerves
mediate normal day-to-day metabolic functions like diges-
tion, resting and making love, the sympathetic nerves are
the 'hawks' of the nervous system. Their message is always

one of "RED ALERT! Prepare for defense — an adaptation is required! *Survival itself is at stake!*"

Who decides that survival itself is at stake? You do. Your decision is carried by electrochemical thought impulses to the hypothalamus, the part of your brain-biocomputer which constantly monitors and programs all the infinitely complex activities of your physical body. The hypothalamus continuously adjusts bodily functions like heart rate, blood pressure, and breathing to conform with the evaluations of your social structure as seen by your intellectual mind. Your message is relayed to heart and blood vessels by two pathways. In the hypothalamus, the aggressive or fearful thought impulse is shunted into the sympathetic nervous system which tells the peripheral blood vessels to constrict as it spurs the heart into a more rapid rate. All this raises blood pressure, preparing the warrior to battle for survival. Neurohormones in the hypothalamus are chemical substances which stimulate the pituitary to secrete hormones commanding the endocrine glands to prepare the body to flee or to fight. Thus we find that Type A people secrete more adrenaline and norepinephrine, the messengers of impending catastrophe.

Like Dr. Friedman, I wonder why that hasn't been considered more prominently as a major cause for the deterioration of heart and arteries. Perhaps since thoughts and attitudes can't be measured, we succumb to the notion that medical science can't do anything about them. Maybe it can't. But you can.

Dr. Meyer Friedman has offered a lucid description of the type of behavior most frequently associated with heart attack. We can try on the shoe and see if it fits. If it does, we can choose to do something about it, or we can ignore it and go on as before — running the risk of killing ourselves with our survival techniques.

We can respond to stress by continuing to worry. The

psyche then will initiate a series of warnings culminating in body breakdown. Observing these effects, we may tell ourselves, "I'm sick." We can call the doctor and say, "Fix my body." This kind of activity presumes that there is another psyche outside my psyche which can cure me. We expect the doctor to initiate a chain of cause and effect which our psyches can observe, experience, and say, "I'm healed." We presume that this outside psyche, the doctor, knows more about our body than our own psyche does. In the constant moment-by-moment struggle for survival, a war waged by 'me' against whatever is 'not-me', we think we've found an ally in the enemy camp who will repair 'my body'. Who's kidding who?

Why can't my own psyche which is me repair my own body which is also me? Whose life is it anyway?

"You are the mosaic maker," says Dr. Selye. The rest is simple logic. You look at life and decide how it is. Then you pay the price or enjoy the benefits. The decision is yours alone.

10 / Security and Suffering

*"Open thy door to that which must go, for the
loss becomes unseemly when obstructed."*
— RABINDRANATH TAGORE (1861–1941)
Fireflies

"SECURITY IS MAN'S deadliest enemy," George Bernard
Shaw once said. Through our five senses, we perceive a
constantly changing, evolving environment. Environment,
that's a perfect word. It means 'the surroundings of the
mind.' We have seen how inappropriate attitudes toward environmental change can lead to body breakdown and disease. Specifically, we've been told by Dr. Meyer Friedman
that the attitudes resulting in the kind of aggressive, competitive behavior exhibited by Type A people frequently
result in heart attack. According to Hans Selye's model,
that would happen in people for whom the heart was the
weakest link in the body system. Other kinds of people who
respond to stress through a filter of worrisome thoughts and
beliefs might be expected to experience other kinds of breakdown. If the core problem is attitudes — thought, beliefs,
and opinions — then the solution seems simple. All we have to
do is change them. Perhaps only the fittest attitudes survive.

Some of us feel that if we can only nail down a piece of
the good life and stand still on it, we can live happily ever
after. But if distress and disease are a function of people's

resistance to the inevitable changes that accompany the flow of life, then the struggle for security may indeed be "man's deadliest enemy." That suggestion is implicit in the research data provided by Dr. Thomas Holmes, a Seattle psychiatrist. Dr. Holmes feels that "the work of Dr. Friedman and his group at San Francisco's Mount Zion Hospital is one of the major advances in the science of medicine of the past quarter century." His own research project concerns the interrelationship between the biological system (the physical body), the psychological system (the psyche), and the sociological system (the environment) as they relate to disease. In contrast to Friedman, who confined his investigations to one specific disease, Holmes, like Selye, is interested in the way in which mind, body, and environment interact to produce the phenomenon of 'just being sick'.

We have already seen how the intellect, surveying the social scene, may arbitrarily decide that survival, life itself, is totally dependent on the constant accumulation of status symbols. Faced with the mind-created threat of non-existence, the terrible void of non-being, the body mobilizes. Spurred into a state of perpetual (chronic) alarm, the physical organism experiences distress, disease, and breakdown. Dr. Holmes was interested in the nature of social events which surround and contribute to this deadly process. What, he wondered, do life events which produce distress have in common? He found that in response to certain life situations, people tend to get multiple diseases involving multiple body systems.

Seventy percent of all sickness strikes a relatively small segment of our population—about thirty percent. There is a small group of people who, according to Holmes, "have more illnesses than anybody, and when they get sick they get sick all over." These patients do not get one disease in one body system. The typical life history of a sickly person inclludes many operations, sexual difficulties, sterility, and respiratory ailments including sinus trouble, allergies, colds, bronchitis, and pneumonia. Characteristically, they also cry a lot.

Since crying spells are such a large part of the lifestyle of these individuals, Dr. Holmes and his associates decided to take one of these spells and subject it to discrete examination. The doctors measured the amount of blood flow, swelling, and secretory activity in the mucous membranes of the nose, as well as the amount of obstruction to the flow of air through the nasal passages.

"Very often," Dr. Holmes recalls, "the 'noxious agent' [producing the physical symptoms] was the mother-in-law." During discussions of what happens during her visits, patients would say things like, "When that woman comes, I'm helpless!" Choosing a time when the person was relatively calm and serene, Holmes would introduce the topic of the mother-in-law, and at the height of the discussion would take a piece of nasal tissue for study under the microscope. The tissue samples showed engorgement and inflammation, demonstrating that non-physical agents like relationships with a mother-in-law, an unsympathetic boss, or financial difficulties can produce pathologic tissue change! When the subject of conversation was shifted, allowing the patient to calm down and think different thoughts, a biopsy taken from the other side showed that the symptoms of respiratory infection had disappeared. Thus we find that thoughts of helplessness and defeat impede the flow of air to the lungs just as frustration and rage block the flow of blood to the heart. Thoughts, like germs and poisons, can induce disease. Eliminate the root cause, the thought, and the disease disappears.

Dr. Holmes refers to his work, done about thirty years ago, as "the modern version of Koch's Postulates." He showed that attitudes toward social events produce distress just as Professor Koch showed that the tubercle bacillus incites tuberculosis. We prove that a germ causes a disease by introducing the agent into a susceptible organism, and demonstrating that this procedure does indeed induce the specific state.

What effect does the mood of the patient have on the course of germ-related illness like tuberculosis? About ten years after his work established the disease-instigating capabilities of social events, Dr. Holmes and his group set out to investigate the relationship between body resistance to bacterial infection and the psychological state, the mood, of the patient. Inflammation is the cardinal reaction of living tissue to invasion by a germ. Cortisone, a hormone secreted by the adrenal gland in response to the stress of infection, is, as you recall, the prototype "hormone of harmonious cooperation." Cortisone combats inflammation. Holmes and his co-workers found that blood levels of cortisone-like hormones and the course of the disease varied with the patient's mood. "We found that as long as patients felt hopeless, withdrawn, apathetic, and overwhelmed, they had very little resistance, and the disease did not get much better. As patients improve in terms of mood and behavior, their adrenal glands put out protective hormones, and they get better."

"If," Holmes continues, "there is a relapse of mood to more depressed, there is a decrease in the level of bodily resistance, as shown by a decrease in the level of blood hormones, and the condition ceases to improve." This happened even though the patients continued to receive high doses of antibiotics! Just as thoughts can induce illness, they determine the relative effectiveness of the body's resistance to infection by germs.

Holmes then began a systematic study of the psychological and social events which precede the onset of illness. Selecting a patient with tuberculosis, he counted the number of residential changes, job changes, etc., from twelve years before the onset of infection up to one year before admission to the hospital with pulmonary tuberculosis. The researchers discovered an increasing frequency of life changes, all requiring adaptive adjustment, "mounting to a crisis, a crescendo, a dramatic concatenation of life changes in the two years immediately preceding admission to the hospital with full blown tuberculosis." Recall the admonition of Dr. Hans Selye: "If you have to adapt, you are under stress."

Does the strain of adapting to life changes consistently lead to disease (tuberculosis in this case) or were the findings merely coincidence? Seeking to clarify this issue, Holmes turned his attention to the staff of a hospital actively involved in treatment of tuberculosis. Working on the wards, each staff member ran an equal risk of coming down with TB. Because of the high exposure rate, each employee was required to have a chest X-ray every three months. Some came down with clinical TB, others did not. What was the difference between the two groups? "The frequency of life change events clearly distinguished the two groups," says Dr. Holmes Those who became sick were found to have a significantly greater number of stressful life change events in the time period immediately preceding the discovery of infection in the lung. "Now we can say," according to psychiatrist Holmes, "that life change clearly precedes the onset of the disease."

The same rule of thumb applies to accidents and injuries. Professional football players are exposed to potential injury situations just as hospital personnel are exposed to infection from patients. Why are some players repeatedly hurt, while others escape unscathed from the fray? Do life change factors play a role? Studying the incidence of injury among University of Washington football team members, Dr. Holmes and his group were able to keep the factors of age, sex, and risk of injury constant. They found that a minority of the players sustained most of the injuries. Comparing the amount of life change undergone by players in the month before the season, Dr. Holmes discovered that, as in the case of tuberculosis, the accident prone minority was characterized by a high incidence of life change.

What is the means by which the stress of adapting to significant life change predisposes one to disease? Holmes theorizes that the amount of life change is perceived by the subject as an overwhelming situation. He or she simple gives up. "The brain," he postulates, "turns off the adrenal cortex which stops producing protective hormone, and the germ, if present, can then do its destructive work." That makes tuberculosis look like a psychosomatic disease, doesn't it?

What about other diseases? What about other kinds of accidents, injuries, and the like? Are some life events more likely to herald the onset of disease, accident, or injury than others?

The method employed to determine the relative value of life events as producers of health changes was derived from a field called *psychophysics*. Working at Harvard University, Dr. S. S. Stevens showed that subjective evaluation of the relative loudness of a group of sounds correlated extremely closely with the actual measured loudness of the test sound. They showed that humans can make highly reliable and reproducible subjective estimations about sensory experiences. What they did was to say to the subject, "Listen to this sound." Introducing a sound of known loudness as a point of comparison, they would then play another sound of different intensity. Listeners were asked to make a subjective evaluation as to whether 'sound one' was louder or softer than 'sound two'. If the sound was louder or softer, they were asked to decide how much louder or softer — twice as loud (soft)? Ten times? A hundred times? Dr. Holmes describes the experiment in this manner: "After comparing 'sound two' with 'sound one', the subjects evaluated the relationship of 'sound three' to 'sound one', 'sound four' to 'sound one', and so on. There was almost perfect agreement between subjective and objective measurement of comparative sound intensity. The louder or softer the sound actually was, the louder or softer it was judged to be."

Applying the same technique to his own research, Dr. Holmes chose marriage as a typical social event requiring a change in adjustment, giving it a value of five hundred 'life change units'. He then asked his subjects, "Does trouble with the boss require more change in adjustment than marriage, or does it require less adaptive change than marriage? If it requires more change in adjustment than marriage, put down a number larger than five hundred. If it requires less change in adjustment, put down a smaller number." How about things like a jail term? "Some people saw a jail term as similar to marriage," quipped Dr. Holmes. In that case they were told to give it a value of five hundred.

About four hundred typical residents of Seattle, representative of the socioeconomic and demographic divisions of the city, were asked to participate in the experiment. In terms of the relative value they assigned to different events, there was almost perfect agreement between the sexes. "We found," reports Holmes, "that Japanese are very much like the Americans, who are like the Peruvians, Spanish, and the French." Poor and rich, old and young, educated and uneducated, the participants universally agreed that a traffic ticket or a vacation requires about one-tenth the amount of adaptive life change as does the death of a spouse, and that marriage requires about half as much change. Dr. Holmes found that people with high life change scores tend to show more illnesses of all sorts compared to people with relatively low life change scores.

Holmes suggests that perhaps pregnancy is related to a mounting crescendo of life change events. Comparing the occurrence of pregnancy in married versus unmarried women in the child bearing age, he found that pregnancy often occurs in a setting of mounting life change. Marriage may or may not be one of the significant life change events contributing to the onset of pregnancy. "Pregnancy," he says, "acts just like a chronic disease. You can get it more than once, it lasts a long time, and it is subject to complications." In order to avoid confusion, therefore, he decided to speak of life changes producing *health changes*.

Pursuing the similarity between pregnancy and other forms of health change, Dr. Holmes tells us that, "Just as some of the people get most of the illnesses, some of the people have most of the pregnancies. Fifty percent of the next generation," he says, "is produced by less than one-sixth of the present generation."

Pregnancy is not simply a matter of the biology of sexual intercourse and its consequences, just as clinical tuberculosis is not a simple matter of the presence of bacteria within the lungs. Germ and sperm are each capable of producing their respective specific health changes, but, like seeds, they can't flower and grow in the absence of fertile soil. Seed, sperm, and germ are necessary but not sufficient for the manifestation of a flower, a child, or an illness.

Psychiatrist Thomas Holmes has shown us a beautiful stone. Another jewel for our mosaic; a mosaic which, as Dr. Selye suggested, "will tell you something about how to live, how to be happy, how to enjoy life." Dr. Holmes has demonstrated that *change is the milieu, the soil in which sickness and suffering flower*. And yet, he tells us that twenty percent of the people in his sample populations experience "an increasing frequency of life changes, mounting to a crisis, a crescendo, a dramatic concatenation of life changes," *and they do not get sick!*

It would seem that those who do not get sick in the midst of cataclysmic life change have better coping techniques. Using Dr. Roberto Assagioli's model, we would postulate that perhaps they do not identify with the status quo, and are therefore not swept away by life's inevitable and perpetual transformations. Flexibility and adaptability seem to play a role in survival. "We would dearly like to know," says Dr. Holmes, "what it is that those twenty percent have, that most of the rest of us don't have." In the case of coronary occlusion, cardiologist Meyer Friedman notices that they have a placid (Type B) attitude toward life and its changes. As neurophysiologist Barbara Brown points out, "The intellect can contrive ways to relieve and to prevent reactions to stress." Maybe the folks in that twenty percent don't get emotionally involved in their own life stories. Stress is the thrust of life itself, evolving new forms in a climate of incessant and inexorable change. Resistance, attachment to the status quo, may indeed be the root of all human suffering, all distress. What we need to do, perhaps, is to let go and feel fine. You could follow Dr. Selye's advice and consider whether dealing with particular life change is worth the risk of getting your catatoxic juices flowing. Dr. Holmes puts it this way: "There are lots of things that are more important [to the eighty percenters] than *not* being sick. One of them is taking a promotion if you consider it to be in your best career interests. If you take the promotion, at least be aware of the risk you are running and be prepared to pay the price of an illness occurring as a by-product of the way you pursue your goals."

PART IV

Transformations

"Enlightenment is the only game in town—if you don't take it seriously."
— ERIC ROLF (Contemporary)

11 / Detachment and Rebirth

*"He who binds to himself a joy doth the winged
life destroy. He who kisses the joy as it flies
lives in eternity's sunrise."*
— WILLIAM BLAKE (1757–1827)

FACE TO FACE with hard scientific evidence that attitudes
toward life events and social changes are, like germs, potentially pathogenic, we find ourselves confronting the mystery
of life itself. Like Narcissus, we grow thirsty and approach
the pool of life to drink — as we must. But unlike Narcissus,
we can avoid grabbing at the image reflected back at us; we
can refuse to drown.

Way back East, a long time ago, an aristocrat named
Gautama set out on a quest. A truly compassionate person,
he sought to uncover the root of human suffering. During a
long and adventurous life, in the course of which he founded
one of humanity's great religions, Gautama Buddha announced his findings.

"Attachment," he theorized, "is the source of all human
suffering."

A reasonable hypothesis. Certainly it's as worthy of
consideration as the one that claims suffering is due to circumstances — to germs, accidents, bad luck, and the like. If
we admit that the thesis, attachment breeds anguish, might
be true, then we have to allow that much suffering — physical,

mental, and emotional — is self-induced. Gautama Buddha's theory implies that the level of suffering you experience is a measure of your refusal to let go of something. Perhaps that's what Christ meant when he said, "Lay not up for yourselves treasures upon earth . . . for where your treasure is, there will your heart be also."

The hypothesis that attachment breeds suffering is easy to put to the test. Use the scientific method. You can test it for yourself without any financial outlay for the purchase of laboratory animals, since you can be your own guinea pig. There's no need to waste time or typing paper applying for a research grant. All the experiment requires is a living human body with a sufficiently open mind to allow that the hypothesis or notion under examination might be true.

The procedure is simple. Choose a minor annoyance in your life, something which is bothering you right now. If you choose a physical problem as your target symptom, do the experiment at the time when your symptoms are present. If, for instance, you have backaches or sinus problems, work with them when they are actively bothering you. *Observe the content of your thinking mind at the time the target symptom forces itself into your conscious awareness.*

A pattern of thought or activity may emerge, a pattern which seems somehow connected with your suffering. You may be surprised to learn that one of your attachments is trying to kill you. As a family physician, I was struck by the observation that many of my patients — especially those with ulcers, back pains, or heart disease — had something in common. Those people were actually killing themselves making a living! Are you?

Think about your job for a moment. Picture yourself at work. Watch your body as you do. Do those thoughts and pictures affect your bodily state right this instant? Try raising the power of the stimulus. Think about losing your job. What would it feel like if you found out right now that YOU'RE FIRED! Contemplating that loss, quickly shift your attention to your body. Shifting attention back and forth between what you're thinking about and how your body feels, note carefully the relationship between the two. Then think about something you like to do better than anything else. Imagine the time you first learned to enjoy it. Recall the smells, the tastes, the feelings. Reproduce the sensations in your body, now. In your mind's eye, and with your mind's ear, recreate the associated sights and sounds. Notice how your body feels as you do that. *Body reflects mind.* For better or for worse, your state of health accurately mirrors the state of your mind.

Dr. Roberto Assagioli, the noted Italian psychiatrist, offered the following situations as examples of suffering induced by attachment to life situations which are, by nature, transient: "an athlete who grows old or loses physical strength; a person whose attractiveness begins to fade with time; a mother whose children have grown up; a student facing graduation and the responsibilities of maturity." In his book *Act of Will,* the late founder of Psychosynthesis wrote, "Such situations can produce painful crises, partial psychologic deaths. No frantic clinging to the old identity can avail. The true solution can only be a 'rebirth' . . . into a new and higher state of being."

"Give it up; let it go," advised Alan Watts, American author and philosopher. That's a nice six-word summary of Dr. Assagioli's 'rebirth' prescription. "Diseases," a colleague of mine once wrote, "are not entities. They are merely different modes of suffering." According to the physicians' *law of parsimony,* the simplest description is always the best. The concept of *energy* gives us a handle on such diverse phenomena as electricity, anger, and the motion of a billiard ball. Clouds, tears, and puddles are all manifestations of the unique substance we call *water. Is it possible that back-*

ache, depression, and heart disease flow from one source: attachment?

The tendency to treat diverse phenomena as aspects of a single concept may be termed *holistic*. The idea, then, that diseases are modes of attachment would be more holistic than the view which sees sickness as a malfunction in a machine composed of isolated organs and cell systems. Let's call the latter approach to disease *atomistic*. The holistic trend in American medical thought is represented today by the concept of *psychosomatic disease*. As we have previously noted, many clinical entities, including asthma, ulcers, and high blood pressure, are triggered by stress and alleviated by stress-reduction techniques such as biofeedback, meditation, and jogging. Those diseases which have a close relationship to mental stress are called psychogenic, or mind-induced. *If you can have mind-induced disease, why not mind-induced health?*

Attachment is derived from our beliefs about survival. Compare the implications of Darwin's theory of survival of the fittest with those in Christ's admonition to "Consider the lilies of the field, how they grow; they toil not, neither do they spin." Which of these survival theories do you believe?

Charles Darwin and philosophers like Thomas Hobbes have pictured a world remarkably similar to the Type A personality described by Dr. Meyer Friedman. Life is a war of all against all, a life or death struggle for survival.

In this perspective, we find ourselves peering out through the skin barrier, deciding that all that stuff which is 'not-me' is somehow competing with me. The only way we can protect ourselves is to possess, dominate, control that which is 'not-me' — to attach ourselves to things and people that serve as a fortress-like barrier between us and the ever threatening outside world. Thus we find ourselves killing germs, conquering nature, and struggling for survival. Existence itself becomes a commodity which is in short supply.

Since there isn't enough to go around, I have to insure my supply by diminishing someone else's.

We don't have to subscribe to the survival of the fittest theory or behave according to its tenets. Medical and psychological research have clearly shown that by incorporating such beliefs into our lives, we find, like the comic strip character Pogo, that "we have met the enemy — and he is us."

Now let's change lenses and see what happens. Suppose we arbitrarily decide that it's all me, that the universe produced me just as a tree produces apples. Neither the tree nor the universe is hostile to the fruit of its existence. Look at the world through this lens; see if it changes your life, relieves anxiety, tension, and generally reduces your suffering. If it works, you'll have learned something new about the way your psyche operates.

Choose a specific timespan during which you will do the experiment. I recommend one week. During that time you will interpret every experience as a lesson which is trying to teach you something. Dissolve all your borders. Presume that each person you meet during this test week is a reflection of you. When someone upsets you or impresses you, write down a list of the characteristics of that person which you find most striking and obvious. Presume that you are reacting to a part of yourself. Look for the lesson in all your encounters. Adjust your thinking and see if your experience improves.

This experiment can help you explore on an experiential or gut level the connection between your mind and body, to help you see for yourself that the two are one and the same, each reflecting and creating the other.

Consider that in order to be born, we had to evolve from the intrauterine to the extrauterine plane of existence, to adapt to the alien land beyond the nourishing material waters, to extract life-giving oxygen from air instead of from water; we learned to take food by mouth instead of through a tube in the navel — and we learned to be afraid. Life on the previous plane, inside mamma, was so simple. Like the lillies of the field, we received life as a gift. We didn't have to work, to plan, or worry. All we had to do was to *be*. Then the plug was pulled. War began. Our nourishing, sustaining maternal universe seemed to turn against us, to attack and attempt to destroy us. Dying to existence in the womb, we were born into existence in the world of time and space. We changed from foetus into child — a fearsome transition indeed. Perhaps we can apply the same perspective to disease processes. We could in a similar manner presume that the force which fuels disease, the growth of a tumor, or a suffocating plaque in an artery wall, is the force of life itself, the force of evolution, of transformation. The force is splitting your shell, pushing you out of your usual life patterns and customary perceptions into the unknown, into the void — just as labor pushes the foetus into a totally new existence. We could let go of our attachment to those beliefs, opinions, and shoulds that prevent us from becoming reborn to a new wholeness.

12 / Making Light of It All

"Thus shall you think of all this fleeting world:
A star at dawn, a bubble in a stream;
A flash of lightning in a summer cloud.
A phantom, an illusion, a dream."
— THE DIAMOND SUTRA

IN the famous allegory of the cave in Plato's *Republic,* the Greek philosopher asks us to imagine a group of people chained since birth in a dark subterranean cavern. They can't move and can't turn around. From behind them a fire casts dim light on a screen that stands in front of the prisoners, while between the fire and the prisoners others parade back and forth carrying figures of men and animals that cast shadow images on the screen. Without any experience of the outside world, the captives would have no choice but to believe that their shadowy realm was the only reality. At this point Plato asks us to consider what would happen if one of the prisoners were freed, shown around the cave, taken outside, then brought back to his fellows. ·Would they believe his explanation of what was going on and what the real world was like? Ordinary sense experience, Plato suggests, is much the same kind of illusion as the shadow images in the cave allegory.

Suppose that human consciousness is like the fire at the rear of Plato's cave, or, to bring the analogy up to date, like a movie projector. Mental images, belief structures, and thoughts would be the film. If we, by the contents of our minds, projected disease or malfunction into our bodies, then the correction would have to be made at the mental level. Drug therapy might alleviate the symptoms or make them disappear temporarily, but that wouldn't get at the root of the problem.

Stanford University physicist Dr. William Tiller compares human experience to a *simulator,* a training device used to teach pilots and astronauts how to operate a plane or spacecraft under actual space-time conditions. Our physical space-time environment is perceived through the five senses, and the mind responds with patterns of thought, belief, and emotion. These patterns form force fields that are projected by the psyche into the physical body and its environment, setting in motion a series of action events. Responding to experience, we adjust the controls to take account of the space-time changes wrought by our psychic activity. That is, we create new patterns that are again reflected by experience.

Dr. Tiller's model is not unlike the Buddhist concept which describes the material world and the observing psyche as two mirrors facing each other. Each reflects and creates the other simultaneously. We create future events by our thoughts, attitudes, and actions just as past events have created our current thoughts, attitudes, and actions.

What we do emerges from what we think, feel, and experience. Dr. Tiller believes that "the larger purpose of human life is the evolution (of the psyche) into higher states of awareness." Consciousness by its mutation imposes change and mutation on the physical body. Your own consciousness was quite different when you were an infant or a small child. As your psyche grew, learned, and evolved, your physical vehicle changed its form. Thus the baby is psychologically and physically different from the teenager who is quite different from the mature adult. "Thinking and doing," says Professor Tiller, "not only reprogram future events but reorganize our structure to be responsive to those events." Just as atoms and molecules precipitate thoughts, emotions, and images; so perhaps thoughts, emotions and images influence quarks, atoms, molecules, and things. Change the thoughts and the body-environment conforms.

In Dr. Tiller's model, "we are all elements of spirit (light), multiplexed elements of the divine." Light, in order to experience perception, becomes the mind. "Mind, in order to have some experience which it can perceive, has to invent a game, a simulator for experience. . . . That's our world of form and appearance." The psyche creates for itself a hologram called 'the real world', and then plays with and within it. Observing its own creation, the light-consciousness decides that the objects in that creation are different, separated from the psyche which now perceives them. That decision creates the illusion or the phenomenon of space-time — the gap between the observer and the observed. Dr. Tiller postulates two aspects of space-time: positive space-time and negative space-time. Let's call the former *objective* and the latter *subjective*. Events perceived in outside, objective space-time are said to be *real,* while events taking place within the mind are said to be *imaginary*. Actually, there may be a reciprocal relationship between the two spaces, each creating and reflecting the other. Dr. Tiller proposes that the purpose of life is evolution. He suggests that we have experiences in order to grow and learn, to become more conscious.

Science has reintroduced magic into our lives. It is now possible to hypothesize the existence of 'mindons', subatomic wave particles emitted by the psyche. Suppose we decide to construct a reality hypothesis which postulates that the mindon is equivalent to the quark — the hypothetical ultimate building block of matter which can theoretically form electrons, protons, atoms, and things, all the way up to your aching back. Let's say that quarks and mindons are identical. That allows us to stay within the bounds of current theory. We could postulate that while the mindon like the quark has no physical existence outside the psyche, still it has the power to create our entire physical reality. That is to say that perhaps our thoughts about the world we experience with our five senses are the basic stuff of that world. Our reality might be crystallized thought. Let's follow this intriguing hypothesis a bit further.

Light exists in two forms according to today's scientific authorities. It performs as a particle when it doesn't happen to be acting like a wave. You, insofar as you are a manifestation of the living light of human consciousness, do the same. Starting the day (or this life) in the wave form, we quickly surround ourselves with an encasing shell of things that 'really matter'. Perhaps sickness is the attempt of your living light to break out of that shell, to struggle free in order to build a more evolved structure, which will in its time also be shed.

The pattern is the same throughout nature. The wave crystallizes into the particle, and begins the struggle to free itself from the confines of rigid, particulate structure. You incarnate every day, only to leave your particular body and social structure every night. Consciouness reverts to the disembodied wave form of existence, sleep.

The experience you have during the day is imprinted or remembered in two ways. On the particle side, the memory is recorded into the physical body. If, for instance, you work too hard, your aching muscles remind you. Genes, as we have seen, are the carriers of inheritance, the arrangement of atoms which instructed the incarnating energy of the universe—as it was making your body—to form two arms, two legs, and a head. On the wave side, your time-space interlude is remembered as fleeting holographic images, echoes of conversations, thoughts about what might have been or what should have been, all accompanied by the ebb and flow of emotion.

Christopher Hill offers the observation that in order to perceive any object you need two kinds of light. You need the light of consciousness — you must be awake and responsive — and you also need a source of 'outside' light to illuminate the matter, mass, or object. If either light source is missing, you will fail to experience the thing under scrutiny.

Compare Hill's observations with those in the Chinese text called *The Secret of the Golden Flower:* "The light is not in the body alone, neither is it only outside the body. Mountains and rivers and the great Earth are lit by sun and moon: all that is this light. Therefore it is not only within the body. Understanding and clarity, knowing and enlightenment, and all motion are likewise this light; therefore it is not just something outside the body."

Atoms emit light. The frequency or color of the light identifies the atomic element which emits it. If we want to identify the elements making up a distant star, we study the colored light emissions from that star — the spectrum. One arrangement of colors says, "I'm lead"; another arrangement says, "I'm copper" or "iron" or "zinc." The spectrum of colors emitted by each atom or compound is a fingerprint identifying that particular substance. It seems reasonable to suggest that the atom, the compound, the *thing,* may be a crystallized, frozen state of the light which it emits. *Perhaps the light, the matter which emits it, and the psyche which perceives it are the same, of one essence.*

We can take this hypothetical exploration a step farther. If, as Einstein's formula $E=MC^2$ suggests, matter and energy are functions of light, and if human consciousness, the psyche, is a function of light, then we are, like the stars, beings of light in our very essence. Perhaps it would be only fair to point out that this hypothesis is a plagiarism. It was first advanced almost two thousand years ago during an event called the Sermon on the Mount when the prophet Jesus Christ told an electrified audience of thousands, "You are the light of the world."

13 / Seeing the Light

"Each of us has as his personal Medicine a particular animal reflection. The characteristics of this reflection are determined by the nature of the animal itself. . . ."
— HYEMEYOHSTS STORM (Contemporary)
Seven Arrows

THERE is a Blackfoot Indian legend which sheds light on our discussion about human consciousness. Newly created onto the planet Earth, lost and bewildered, our primal parents prayed for guidance and direction. The Great Spirit replied that they were to watch for the appearance of animals in their dreams. "These creatures," said the Great Spirit, "will be your guides and allies." From the dream creatures, says the myth, they learned to build shelters and received instructions on making fires, planting corn, and the art of hunting.

Is there actually a difference between the holograms we call dreams, hallucinations, and visions, as opposed to those we call time-space, things, or events? Are the 'allies' of Don Juan or the 'voices' of the prophets still available to you and me? In order to illuminate these questions, I'd like to describe an experiment performed at a University of California Extension seminar at Santa Cruz involving about fifteen hundred people. If you like, you can try the procedure and find out for yourself if there is any validity to the premise proposed by the Blackfoot Indian myth. The procedure I am about to describe is an *algorhythm,* a series of steps by means of which you can elicit the solution to a problem by summoning assistance from your biocomputer, your three-million-year-old, one-hundred-billion-cell human brain.

Operating Your Biocomputer
(How to summon your ally)

1. Find a safe place where you won't be disturbed.
2. Get comfortable (loose belt, tie, bra, etc.).
3. Close your eyes.
4. Shift attention from thoughts to breathing. As you inhale, count to yourself: "1000, 2000, 3000, 4000." Begin to breathe in at the count of "one thousand," and finish each breath by the count of "four thousand." Time your exhalation the same way — as you release your breath, count backwards: "4000, 3000, 2000, 1000." After the breath leaves your body with the count "1000," begin the cycle again with inhalation. Count slowly so that each number represents one second of elapsed time.
5. As you inhale, imagine a current or wave of energy being drawn up the front of your body, reaching the top of your head with the count of "4000." As you exhale, sense the energy wave or flow curving over the top of your head to sink slowly down the back of your body, leaving your heels and entering the ground at the end of exhalation. Grounding the energy is very important to the procedure.
6. Think of the most beautiful place you can imagine and pretend you are there. Mentally create the sounds, the smells, and the body sensations appropriate to being in that place. Continue steps one through six for about fifteen minutes.

7. In your mind's eye, as you continue the previous steps, look around casually. You may be surprised to see or otherwise sense the presence of a living creature — a person, an animal, a plant — something which lives in the place you have recalled. Some people see the sun, the moon, or even lights. Others are merely aware of a silent voice responding to them. It may be a holographic representation of a person or animal you know in time-space, or it may be a life form which is endemic to the space you have chosen. At the beach you may see a bird, fish, or dolphin. In the forest you may meet a deer, squirrel, lion, or anything else that normally lives in that habitat. (This creature is your ally, your guide and advisor; your psychoanalyst, if you will. A hologram printed out by your biocomputer, which pops spontaneously into your empty awareness. If you happen to meet a life form which frightens you, such as an alligator or a monster, instantly image it behind an impenetrable barrier.)

8. Befriend your guide in the best manner you know. Feed it, pet it, ask its name; find out if it's male or female. You may be surprised to see a fearful monster turn into a handsome prince or into a beautiful damsel. Remember that, since this is your fantasy, you are in complete charge.

9. Ask your guide if he or she is willing to meet with you for fifteen minutes daily for a period of one week. (They always agree.)

10. In return for your offering, and to seal your agreement, ask your ally to demonstrate a sign of its power. This may be immediate relief of a physical symptom or an answer to a thorny life problem.

In order to tap the information stored in your inherited biocomputer, it is helpful but not necessary to make a visual image. The printout is often in thought. Many, like Albert Einstein, receive information from the computer in the form of ideas and inspirations. As some of my patients have reported, you may feel as if you're talking to yourself. You are, and that's not important. You're talking to a part of yourself which is veiled to your ordinary state of consciousness.

If you would like to experience body revitalization, follow steps one through six for fifteen minutes daily over a period of seven consecutive days. Note carefully how your body feels when you start the exercise. *Watch for, and make note of the type and degree of improvement or change you notice after you finish.* It helps to keep a notebook or diary.

In the remaining steps your holographic ally tells you why you made your illness and suggests specific life transformations which will initiate the healing process. You may test this phenomenon for yourself by proceeding with steps seven through ten. This subject is discussed in further detail, including case illustrations, in my previous works. The method is an adaptation of Carl Jung's method of active imagination, as described in Volume 14 of his Collected Works.

The entire process is intimately connected with your breathing. Speak to your holographic ally as you exhale to the count of 4000, 3000, 2000, 1000. You need not speak aloud. As you begin your inhalation to the mental count of 1000, 2000, etc., the answer from your computer, your hologram, your ally — God, if you will — simply and silently enters your empty, open awareness. For those who do not yet visualize, the process may first take place as a series of silent thoughts without pictures — like radio instead of TV. If at first you don't *see* a three-dimensional color hologram with your mind's eye, you will *hear* your ally with your mind's ear. In either case, thoughts passing through your mind when you breathe out are yours. Thoughts and ideas entering your mind as you breathe in are computer printouts. Inspirational messages, you might say. Whenever you get an unexpectedly helpful and illuminating idea, you can presume that you received a computer printout of a message from the infinite universe — or the psyche at its center. You can presume the same if you find yourself sick, depressed, or frustrated.

Allow me to share two experiences. "There I was," wrote a participant in the experiment at UCSC, "fifteen hundred people around me, circulating energy and breathing, when I distinctly saw a coyote in my imaginary forest. I asked her name, and the word 'Sheba' flashed into my mind. I petted her, fed her, and we agreed to meet on the back porch of my house at a specified time for fifteen minutes every day for the next week. The following day I went out onto the porch to get comfortable and to begin my meditation. I looked over the rail down into the canyon below the house. There, standing silently, watching me intently, was a female coyote. I had never seen a coyote in that canyon before. I wondered if it might be Sheba."

A coincidence? Undoubtedly. A materialization? Possibly. A patient in my office was rewarded during her meditation by the appearance of a hologram in the form of a lizard named Louis. She met with Louis faithfully for one week, and with his help worked out a difficult family problem. Her husband describes what followed: "Things went quite well for a while, so she gradually gave up the procedure. New problems arose, and she got progressively more agitated and upset. One night, coming home after a particularly distressing evening, she remarked that she was at her wit's end and would freak out if she didn't get some help. As she said this, she turned on the light in the living room, and there in the middle of the rug, staring intently into her eyes, was a lizard!"

These episodes seem to be a gross violation of the law of cause and effect. There is no way, according to our current conventional wisdom, for the mental image of an animal to cause the physical appearance of that animal in four-dimensional space-time. Or is there? "The same living reality," postulated Carl Jung, "was expressing itself in two forms." That living reality is, according to authorities, light. Physical events can be looked at in two ways, according to Dr. Jung. One side believes that every event has a cause, but no purpose. Others maintain that the force driving physical events is intelligent, conscious, and purposeful. Insofar as events are purposeful, they can't be the blind effects of mindless causes.

Let's examine a case history which will illustrate and clarify this important point. A patient consulted me for help in dealing with a condition which had been diagnosed as cancer of the tissues around the mouth and cheek. The tumor was growing rapidly so that one side of his face was swollen. I guided him from steps one through five, the relaxation portion of the procedure, and we stopped. Interestingly, the ally appeared without being actually summoned.

When I asked him to tell me what his face felt like, the patient replied, "It feels like a hand is clutching my face. The fingernails are dug into my cheek and jaw."

"Is it a man's hand or a woman's hand?"

"A woman's. It's definitely a woman's hand."

"Can you step back and, in your mind's eye, see the woman?"

"My God, there she is. I see her!"

"Ask her why she is clawing at your face."

"She says that if I don't sell my antique store, she is going to rip my head off!"

The patient then told me that he operated an antique shop in a once proud urban neighborhood which had become a slum. "I can't get myself to give it up," he revealed, "but the strain is terrible; there's always the possibility of violence." He spent an hour negotiating the matter with the imaginary woman, but his hologram was adamant. She stuck tenaciously to her original demand. "If you don't sell that damned antique shop, I'll rip your head off!"

"Ask her to demonstrate her power," I suggested. "Ask her to relieve your symptoms immediately. Tell her to let go of your head and grant you some relief." As a sign of her power, the lady in the psyche of the antique dealer agreed to relax her grip, "but only for a little while." As he saw her release her hold, he noticed that the swelling in his cheek began to recede to the point where he could once again open his mouth. He left feeling greatly improved. About six weeks later, I received a letter from him which read as follows: "My swelling is back and I'm feeling worse. What did I do wrong?"

"Did you sell your antique shop?" I inquired in my response. He did not reply.

Well-being depends on freedom, which in turn is based on the willingness to let go of attachments, to die to the old and face rebirth. The death required in this case was the ego-death of the antique dealer. Abandoning the business where he always made his living represented for this man a psychological death, a prospect more terrifying than the threat of physical death. Giving up the antique store, dying to all that went before, seemed in this case to be the price for survival.

Another enlightening case history involved a patient selected at random from a colleague's busy general medical practice. Thirty years old, she was referred to my office to see if I could help her deal with a burning sensation in her pelvis which had persisted since she was eighteen — a period of twelve years. Repeated examinations and laboratory tests always led to the same diagnosis: nonspecific urethritis and nonspecific vaginitis. That's medical jargon for inflammation of the urethra and of the vagina for unknown reasons — your guess is as good as mine. The inflammation extended into her bladder and also involved her ovaries and ducts. This woman was at the end of her rope — willing to try anything. She had recruited enormous numbers of drugs, douches, and doctors in her twelve-year search for relief. None worked. The burning was constant and severe.

"Would you like to try something else?" I asked, pleasantly. "What do you mean, something else?" she responded suspiciously. "Lie down on the couch and close your eyes," I said. Her eyes narrowed. "Are you going to do one of those weird mind trips on me?" she demanded. "The trouble is in my pelvis, not in my head!"

The patient was a hard core materialist, unshakable in her belief structure. When I advised her that the only traditional technological medical approach to her problem was to find a specialist who would stretch her urethra to break up scar tissue, she said, "I already did that. I told you I've tried everything."

"You haven't tried controlled breathing," I observed. She was an intelligent person with a no-nonsense approach to life and reality. "I'll do anything that seems reasonable," she insisted, "but I draw the line at mystical mind games."

"Breathing is no mystical game," I countered. "When a person with a chronic ailment is in pain or discomfort for a long time, the body tends to tense up, hunch over, and to restrict breathing." I pointed out that her breathing was indeed quite shallow. She accepted the notion that relaxing and increasing the amount of air taken in with each breath would raise the oxygen level in her lungs. She admitted that an increase in available oxygen might expedite her body's task of recovery and repair. This was a model she could understand and accept. She was willing to try, to observe the results with an open mind.

"What does your symptom feel like?" I asked as she lay on the treatment table doing her breathing exercises. "It feels like there's a fire in my pelvis." she replied. Grudgingly, she agreed to imagine energy circulating up the front of her body with inhalation and down the back of her body with exhalation. I suggested that she think of the energy as ice water. The freezing water circulated through the fire in her pelvis, up the front of her body, over her head, down her back, out her heels, into the bay, and out with the tide. After performing this procedure for about fifteen minutes, she reported that her symptoms were definitely improved. The burning continued with undiminished intensity, but it encompassed a much smaller area in her pelvis. Close attention to a symptom alters that phenomenon. People usually say, "It still hurts," paying no mind to alterations in size and intensity of the painful experience. *Looking for improvement induces improvement.*

Advised to repeat this procedure fifteen minutes thrice daily for one week, she returned the following week for an evaluation of her progress. "Listen, I have to talk to you," she said quietly. "If I tell this experience to my friends, they'll think I'm crazy. Is it possible to go into a hypnotic trance using this technique?" I replied that it was indeed possible. She'd had an intense experience which violated her view of reality. The idea that she was hyponotized and not crazy seemed to set her mind at ease. The word 'hypnosis' made it okay for her to have had the experience.

"Well," she said in hushed tones, "I was sitting there breathing and imagining cold water flushing through my pelvis when suddenly the room disappeared! I felt like I had no physical body. I was just awake and aware, and had no other sensation of physical place or form. [The Maharishi Mahesh Yogi calls this the state of 'unbounded awareness.'] Gradually, I became aware of a flickering yellow light," she continued. "It was like a dream, only I was wide awake. It seemed that I was sitting next to a bonfire."

"Did you see a living creature?" I asked.

"Yes," she replied. "Sitting beside me was a coyote. I remembered what you told me, so I treated the coyote as if

it were real, and I assumed that she was there to help me."
The coyote told her that she was about to have an experience which would be related to the fire in her body. "Don't
be afraid; I'll be with you," said the creature. "As she said
that," continued the patient, "I sensed that I was sitting at
a campfire surrounded by a group of dancing Indians. The
coyote was sitting beside me. I then became aware of the
sensation of being bound with ropes, and I realized that
these were not friendly Indians." Captive to a hostile tribe,
she experienced being gang-raped and murdered by the
dancing warriors. "At the instant of my death," she reported, tears streaming down her cheeks, "I woke up and
was back in my body in my room, only my pain was completely gone, and hasn't returned since. Do you believe in
reincarnation? Do you think that really happened to me in
another lifetime?"

It doesn't matter. Any explanation is as good as any
other. William James said, "Our normal waking consciousness is but one special type of consciousness, while all about
it, parted from it by the filmiest of screens, there lie potential forms of consciousness entirely different. We may go
through life without suspecting their existence, but apply
the requisite stimulus and at a touch they are there in all
their completeness." The vision experienced by our lady
with the burning pelvis falls under the different form of
consciousness as described by James.

Releasing her attachment to the belief that "draws a
line at weird mystical mind games," she allowed and experienced a vision which brought an end to her suffering.
Will it work for you? Try it and see.

14 / Endings and Beginnings

*"True end is not in the reaching of the limit
but in a completion which is limitless."*
— RABINDRANATH TAGORE (1861–1941)
Fireflys

"THE PROBLEM isn't one of transformation," author Eric
Rolf told me while I was visiting his home on the island
of Maui. "The secret of well-being is freedom. The secret
of freedom is the willingness to accept death."

Given society's current attitude toward death, how do
we achieve well-being?

Compare Gautama Buddha's teaching that attach-
ment is the root of suffering with Eric's insight, and we find
that they complement each other. They form an internally
consistent matrix of ideas. The emerging group of operating
hypotheses can be listed as follows:

1. Attachment is the source of all human suffering.
2. Freedom is the key to well-being.
3. The secret of freedom is detachment, the willingness to
   accept loss — even of life.

If it is possible that consciousness, like energy, can be
neither created nor destroyed, then what is death?

There's a story about a famous and well-loved guru

who was approaching the end of his allotted time on earth. As death drew near, his assembled disciples began to weep and shout loudly, "Don't go, guru. Please don't depart from us, we need your guidance and your light." Raising himself up on his elbow, the guru uttered the following words with his last breath: "Don't be silly. Where could I possibly go?"

We have observed that the human body is often regarded as it it were a thing in space. We have also, perhaps erroneously, considered death to be a pathologic entity. Many in the scientific community presume that in order to enhance life we must eliminate death. 'Death to death' is the battle cry of the cryogenicists. They are the folks who will freeze and preserve your mortal remains until such time as someone figures out a remedy for whatever it is that killed you; then they will bring you back to life.

"Sometimes, I wonder why we in the helping professions make such a big nightmare out of death and dying." So says Dr. Elisabeth Kübler-Ross, a psychiatrist who has specialized in the care of the terminally ill for the past two decades. By prolonging life at all costs, we proceed on the assumption that the human consists only of the physical body. The implications of Dr. Kübler-Ross's work suggest that you are an immortal consciousness inhabiting a transient physical form. Our present-day scientific understanding of the human phenomenon is limited, she feels.

What is this event we call death? Perhaps it's merely a transition as Dr. Kübler-Ross suggests. "When you watch dying patients," she recalls, "when you have a deep personal relationship with another person; when you touch them, talk to them, and you look into each other's eyes — and a moment later they are dead — the corpse lying in the bed seems to me like an old winter coat, cast aside in the spring when there is no more use for it."

Her research shows that people tend to die in character. Some pass away with peace and dignity. "Fighters and rebels die fighting and rebelling, chronic deniers die in denial," she reports. Shock, denial, anger, depression, and bargaining may become manifest during the stages of dying — triggered by fear, fear of the unknown. That fear is derived from attitudes and beliefs developed from the experience of life. In a well-known poem by Dylan Thomas, the last two lines implore,

> Do not go gentle into that good night.
> Rage, rage against the dying of the light.

He's talking about the chronic fighter, rebelling even at the moment of death. "Sitting with dying children, you begin to see what *life* is," Dr. Kübler-Ross points out.

"When you have learned to see the joys, pains, and sorrows of life, not as chance happenings, and certainly not as a punishment from God, but as gifts," says this tiny woman whose intimacy with death has taught her much, "you can learn, grow, become less attached, and become aware of the fact that nothing, but *nothing* belongs to you." If you know this, she believes, "then you cannot be afraid of death and dying anymore."

There is a meaning to suffering, Dr. Kübler-Ross believes. The syndrome of shock, denial, anger, depression, and bargaining is not unique to death, but is frequently found to accompany the painful experiences of life. People whose lives are marked by tragedy and loss go through the experiences of dying with each catastrophe, large and small. Loss is equated with death insofar as we identify or become attached to that which we are forced to give up. Dr. Kübler-Ross calls such experiences 'little deaths'.

"If you lose your vision," she observes, "or become paraplegic; if you lose your pet or your home; if you're in the process of separation or divorce; if you lose your boyfriend or girlfriend — some people, even if they only lose their contact lenses, go through the stages of dying." People who have suffered many of these little deaths can accept loss of life, the space-time experience, with equanimity and peace — even with relief. "All people," claims Dr. Kübler-Ross, "have to go through many 'little deaths' before the final death. Little deaths are really lessons in letting go."

Recall Gautama Buddha's teaching, "Attachment is the source of all human suffering." Perhaps the little deaths described by Dr. Kübler-Ross, expanded to include illness and accidents, represent promptings from the psyche to renew our commitment to freedom, to shed the winter coat of attachments that hinder new growth. Born free, we can choose to give up that freedom. That's what free will is all about. No one can take that power of choice away from you, and no one can give it to you. There is a meaning to suffering; death is a necessary prelude to rebirth and renewed life.

In her book *Woman's Mysteries,* Esther Harding wrote, "The ego, the conscious personality dies. We do not know and cannot even guess what happens to the 'doer', the 'creator' behind the scenes." Some of Dr. Kübler-Ross's patients have 'returned' after being pronouced clinically dead to shed light on this mystery. Many of those who were approaching their final hours with peace and dignity reported a common occurrence before dying. They told Dr. Kübler-Ross that they were in communication with a dead relative. Delusions? Hallucinations? The phenomenon is, according to Dr. Kübler-Ross, much too real for her to be satisfied with a mere label. Another commonly reported phenomenon is the separation of consciousness from the dying body.

A critically ill patient, admitted to the intensive care unit of a small hospital in Indiana, was pronounced clinically dead. As the woman reported after reviving, she became aware of the sensation of floating out of her physical body, hovering over the bed, and watching with great interest the attempts to bring her back to life. "She watched the resuscitation attempts on her corpse with great amazement," reports Dr. Kübler-Ross. "Afterwards, she was able to tell us who came in first, who came in last, what they wore, and what they said." During the frantic attempts to snatch her from the jaws of death, the patient had a strong urge to communicate with the frenetically scurrying resuscitation team down below. She wanted to tell them, "Cool it, take it easy, relax, it's all right." She soon realized that although she could perceive them, communication was impossible. "Finally," the patient said later, "I gave up on them and lapsed into unconsciousness." All this, according to her attending physician, occurred in a forty-five minute period during which she had no vital signs at all!

Dr. Carl Jung, another psychiatrist interested in the phenomenon of human consciousness, has also reported total separations between psyche and unconscious body. In one instance a post-partum woman who hemorrhaged and became unconscious had the sensation of floating up onto the ceiling, and watched the attempts to revive her. Afterwards, she was able to repeat whole conversations overheard as she lay unconscious at the brink of death.

Now that, dear reader, is clinical data, reported by reputable, well-trained physicians. It is also paranormal, mystical, and weird. That doesn't mean we should assume that it didn't happen, but certainly this data will make no sense to anyone who has a mechanistic view of human life. From a purely phenomenological point of view, that is, by merely describing what happened in simple terms, we might suggest that the moribund patients switched channels. Where did they get the information that we thought only came with rational consciousness? To which other channel did they switch?

For the mechanistically inclined, there is a rational hypothesis, or explanation if you will. Dr. Jung suggests that the autonomic nervous system, the network consisting of the spinal cord and its myriad extensions, could have transmitted messages which gave his clinically dead patient the sensation of continuing consciousness. One might even suggest that the ninety billion glial cells which support the thirteen billion 'functioning' brain cells can transmit consciousness and information to an apparently dead person. Dr. Kübler-Ross offers us a simple hypothesis. "Human beings," she theorizes, "consist of more than just a physical body." She has accumulated a significant number of case histories, other than the one cited previously, to give substance to her claim. All were persons who lacked any vital signs or who were pronounced clinically dead, but who were revived and returned to life.

All said that they remained fully conscious at the moment of death. They were fully aware of themselves and experienced the sensation of floating out of their physical bodies. This observation has considerable support in the literature. *The Tibetan Book of the Dead* (an ancient guide to transition) informs us, for example, that it takes a while for a person to realize that he or she is really dead.

After clinical death and subjective separation, Dr. Kübler-Ross's patients report a feeling much like that of a butterfly coming out of a cocoon. They are in full possession of their faculties and able to perceive everything that is going on around their bodies. At that time there is a great feeling of well-being, "a feeling of serenity, freedom, and peace." Many patients were angry at the medical teams for forcing them out of that blissful state. In their physical bodies they were again vulnerable to pain and suffering. (Similar cases and some theorizings are to be found in my book *Time, Space, and the Mind* and in Raymond A. Moody's *Life After Life*.) Many who have been brought back from clinical death find themselves patiently waiting for a return to that state which they describe as full of beauty, peace, freedom — a state of well-being.

15 / Survival — The Leap of Faith

"Perfect speed, my son, is being there."
— RICHARD BACH (Contemporary)
Jonathan Livingston Seagull

DEATH, as Dr. Elisabeth Kübler-Ross has shown us, may not be the problem. Perhaps survival is the problem, at least for those beset with worry, anxiety, and fear. The fact that many patients who returned from 'death' were angry with the resuscitation teams for forcing them out of a blissful state speaks for itself. Yet, if freedom is the key to well-being, and the secret of freedom is detachment, the willingness to accept death, then a joyful life filled with a sense of purpose and well-being is possible.

Medical and psychological research has clearly isolated certain attitudes as potentially pathological, but at that point the path of science disappears into a labyrinth of theoretical ruminations. "Reaching the point where nature refuses to divulge her secret, the scientist turns to philosophy," according to Dr. Max Parrott. Perhaps we would do well to follow his lead.

There are no machines or yardsticks which can measure attitudes, ways of seeing and being in the world. Deprived of measuring machines, the thoroughly objective scientist is immobilized, neutralized, and helpless, like a turtle on its back. Human consciousness is the immeasurable psyche. The Greek word *psyche* means, Professor Peter Koestenbaum tells us, "that part of our inwardness, our subjectivity, our consciousness, which endures, *which continues after death.*" Since most physicians and psychologists vehemently deny the very existence of the psyche as he defines it, the Professor seems to have a clear field.

The basic problem, which we see manifest in the psychological and medical sphere, is, according to Dr. Koestenbaum, a philosophic problem. The philosophic factor which drives humans to kill and maim their physical bodies in pursuit of status and security is, he says, "the anxiety of nothingness, a universal part of the human condition." Specifically, he tells us that, "The underlying issue to which you must address yourself, with which you must come to grips, is the anxiety about the possibility of non-being." Consciousness cannot contemplate its own extinction. Anxiety is the smoke alarm which indicates to your psyche that you are suffocating, becoming unconscious, in your struggle for security and status quo.

Anxiety, like stress, is a force, an energy. Anxiety is the harbinger of change. Properly interpreted it feels like vigor, vitality, and excitement. Dr. Koestenbaum sees repression and denial of the specifically human force of anxiety as the denial of our own human nature, as that which leads to distress, sickness, and suffering. "The denial of life, the destruction of the excitement of human growth and creativity leads to the formation of symptoms." What does anxiety have to teach us? How can we use these revelations to improve the quality of our life experience?

Anxiety, the empty, hollow feeling in our deep inside self wells up from time to time of its own accord to remind us that nothing lasts. As we struggle with determination toward our chosen goal, perhaps at the pinnacle of success, the message, the handwriting on the wall, reminds us that

"This Too Shall Pass." Not only that, but our continued existence into the next instant is at the mercy of agencies over which we have no control and questionable influence. Koestenbaum uses a medieval Christian image to highlight his view of our basic human situation: "I am a creature. I am created. I exist only because of God's continual creation of me. If God were but for the flicker of a second to cease creating me, my existence would cease."

Those who believe in mindless, mechanical, material evolution are in a similar situation. They count their next heartbeat at the whim of a fifteen-billion-year-old chain of cause and effect which created them accidentally and without love. Regardless of the intellectual trappings, we may each experience the same yawning, infinitely empty abyss within; the abyss of imminent extinction of consciousness — death, the dissolution of form.

Dr. Koestenbaum further expands his theory in the following terms: "The central revelation of anxiety, in addition to the emptiness upon which we rest, is the knowledge of the enormity of our freedom: to define who we are, to choose our values, to choose to be moral, to choose to be immoral, to choose to be loving, to choose to be indifferent, to choose to say 'yes' to life, to choose to say 'no' to life. The problems of society must ultimately be understood in terms of the fact that human beings are free."

Man was created in God's image; like God, a creator, capable of bringing about a reality *ex nihilo,* out of nothing. We, created in his image, are able to create a self-definition, a self-concept, a value system out of nothing.

"Imagine you are standing on the Golden Gate Bridge. What do you experience," Dr. Koestenbaum asks, "as you look down into the bay beneath? You experience," he answers,"... how close you are to non-being, to nothingness. You also experience your freedom because now you are choosing to jump or not to jump. You are in the most original, primaeval, primordial state of being; a state in which you can choose life or you can choose non-life. Looking down into the abyss, you experience the anxiety of non-being, the anxiety of freedom." All that keeps you from annihilation and nothingness is your own decision. You *could* jump, you know.

Sometimes, some of us *do* jump. James Joyce jumped when he renounced Roman Catholicism. The French artist Gauguin jumped when he left a lucrative stock business to set out for the dark unknown of the South Pacific. Getting a divorce, running away from home, any act which constitutes leaving the safe, secure known is a leap into nothingness, an ego-death. Many deliberately suspend themselves over the edge of the abyss. Mountain climbers, sky divers, and other devotees of dangerous sports, says our philosopher, "... work through and cope with the anxiety of nothingness and freedom. When you are hanging on a cliff, the experience of holding on is the experience of choosing *to be*. Why is it," he asks, "... that people are so exhilarated doing an asinine thing like hanging from a cliff? They are exhilarated because they are experiencing in the flesh, a fundamental philosophic truth." The fact is that your conscious beingness, your continued existence, hangs by a very thin thread.

There appears to be a pair of complementary opposite approaches to our exquisitely human predicament. You could grit your teeth and set your will against the vast nothingness which created you, nourishes you, and threatens to annihilate you. Many make the decision that "I will survive, no matter what it takes." Often they decide that it takes unlimited amounts of power, prestige, and material possessions. This approach to the human dilemma is classified by Koestenbaum as *the atheistic solution*. The philosophy he describes is reflected in the biological sciences as the theory of the survival of the fittest. This theory holds that species survival is the prize in a fiercely competitive struggle for existence. Dr. Friedman's description of Type A behavior reflects this philosophical life approach into the field of human behavior and into medicine. One can, on the other hand, surrender to the abyss. *The theistic solution,* says Koestenbaum, "is the solution of faith in which you leap and abandon yourself to the abyss. You trust that the nothingness of the abyss into which you freely leap will support and sustain you. Only after you have leapt will you understand and believe this. This is the religious solution to the problem of anxiety."

Sky diving offers another illustration of the theistic solution. Standing in the open door of an airplane, you face the abyss. Now you choose, out of nothing, to make what the philosopher Kierkegaard called 'a leap of faith'. Reaching a speed of 130 miles per hour, the sky diver discovers that the air will support him or her, and for about one or two minutes, he or she can maneuver like a bird. The thrill, says Koestenbaum, is due to the fact that "you are experiencing in your body one of the most profoundly important philosophical realities of human existence." Having leapt, you find the universe sustains you.

If I were to ask you, "How do you feel right at this moment?" you might shift your attention away from the page and notice among other things the fact that you are still alive. You have survived. You exist. "As of this instant, I've made it." You can say that with complete assurance. You might even feel like the sky diver who, having made the great leap of faith, finds that the universe has provided an invisible cushion of air which absorbs the inexorable force of gravity, slowing the descent.

And then they pull the rip cord to open the parachute. Why do they do that? The leap of faith was a limited leap. It was a leap to the *edge* of extinction. A voyeur's sneaky peak over the brink — a joyous game of tag with a friendly,

Seconds From Death— Then Paratrooper Falls On Another Man's Chute

Paratrooper Jerry Tindal tumbled from the plane, felt the wind tugging at his body as he plummeted toward the earth and counted off four seconds, bracing himself for the expected jerk of his parachute opening.

It didn't open. Falling faster now, Tindal pulled the rip cord on his reserve chute at about 1,100 feet—but that also failed to open.

At almost the same second that he yanked futilely at his rip cord, Tindal landed on top of one of the parachutes of the men who had jumped before him, during a training mission last December 15 at Fort Bragg, N.C.

"Hey, man, get off my parachute," hollered Pvt. Nelson Peters, Tindal's buddy in the 82nd Airborne Division.

Tindal recalled: "That might sound kind of funny, but he just didn't know what was wrong. When he realized what the trouble was, he shouted: 'Come on down!'"

Struggling desperately to keep from slipping away and falling to his death, Tindal grabbed hold of Peters' parachute lines and began sliding down them.

"We were swinging around a lot, and I was getting tangled in my equipment," Tindal remembered. "Then suddenly I thought it was all over.

"I started falling. I went flying right down past Nelson. But he managed to get hold of part of my equipment and stop me.

"He then hauled me back up and grabbed me.

"Man, we got a grip on each other, just clinging on! We sure weren't about to let go then," Tindal said.

"All this was happening real fast. You are thinking of what to do for the best. Yet at the same time you surprise yourself.

"I remember thinking: 'I'm gonna be dead.' And then the thought ran through my mind that if I died I'd miss a noncommissioned officers' course that had been scheduled.

"It was all happening in seconds. You know that the ground is getting close, fast. Then we hit the ground, still holding on to each other. We were so happy, we started screaming.

"We thanked God. I said: 'Hey, man, you saved my life. What can I do for you?' And do you know what Nelson said? He replied: 'Come to church with me.' And here I'd been thinking of having a few beers to celebrate the fact that I was still alive. Now I do say a few words to God, especially before going on a jump," Tindal added.

Peters said: "I am a religious man. I said a prayer of thanks to God and began to cry."

Their battery commander, Capt. Burt A. Vanderchute 2d, commenting on Tindal's cool action in the face of danger, said:

"You have to quickly weigh up all the things you have been taught and come up with the right decision—which is what these fellows did."

playful universe. If your chute fails, you're 'it'! What would you think about on the way down? How would you pass the eternity of time between parachute failure and impact? There is time for your memory tape to activate so that your whole life seems to pass in front of your eyes. At any instant during the descent it is possible to say, "So far, so good, I continue to exist."

The sky diver, you, and I are all in the same situation. Checking our status in the here and now, we find that we are totally alive even as we hurtle toward annihilation. We move at differing velocities. The open parachute merely slows the pace. Instead of bodily disintegration at ground zero, you gently reenter the world of measured time and finite space. You survive.

Even if you survive, you will die sooner or later. If the parachute fails, you lose the opportunity to grow old and weak and sick before you die. So why live at all? That's a question we mostly ignore during the day-to-day progression of our particular life story. Our chain of reasoning is conscious down to the level where the answer to the question "Why am I doing this?" is "To survive! If I don't do this disagreeable thing, I won't be able to live."

We make conscious compromises to insure day-to-day survival. Only when we pull the cord to open the parachute or when we perform a similar act to directly prevent imminent death, do we become aware of our instinctive and insatiable urge to survive, to continue to exist in the face of certain death. Even while we flirt with death we remain hopelessly attached to life.

Attachment to existence breeds suffering in a reality in which everything ends. Judaeo-Christian and other religions seek to assuage our existential anguish. They assure us that our immortal soul, the psyche, exists eternally. If one really believes that, it helps some on the way down. The name of the game, it is often said, is survival. Survival in-

Parachute, Longest Fall Without Parachute. The greatest altitude from which anyone has bailed out without a parachute and survived is 21,980 feet. This occurred in January, 1942, when Lt. (now Lt.-Col.) I. M. Chisov (U.S.S.R.) fell from an Ilyushin 4 which had been severly damaged. He struck the ground a glancing blow on the edge of a snow-covered ravine and slid to the bottom. The human body reaches 99 per cent of its low-level terminal velocity after falling 1,880 feet. This is 117–125 m.p.h. at normal atmospheric pressure in a random posture, but up to 185 m.p.h. in a head-down position.

Vesna Vulovic, 23, a Jugoslavenski Aerotransport hostess, survived when her DC-9 blew up at 33,330 feet over the Czechoslovak village of Ceska Kamenice on January 26, 1972.

— GUINNESS BOOK OF RECORDS

---

stinct is the elemental desire for continued existence in a perpetually transforming reality. It colors our emotions, thoughts, and actions.

It is the fear of death which limits our ability to live fully. Free falling without a parachute, which all of us are in a sense doing, the Type A existence junkie would worry, kick, and scream all the way down (as most of them do). There are also those among us who enjoy the ride, proving that the willingness to accept death is indeed rewarded by well-being. If my life hangs by a thread, I might as well enjoy it while I still have it.

Psychiatrist Dr. Hubert Benoit in his book *The Supreme Doctrine* agrees with Dr. Koestenbaum that we sacrifice our well-being at any given moment when we worry about the possibility of non-being in the next moment. How do we deal with the problem? How do we achieve continuous well-being in a situation in which everything, even life itself, is transient and temporary? Like the falling sky diver, we could check our state of existence at any instant during the descent and say happily, "So far, so good!"

There is a story about Albert Einstein's view of human existence. Asked to pose the most vital question facing humanity, he replied, "Is the universe friendly?" It's possible that the universe knows what it's doing and means you no harm. If you merely consider that possibility, and keep it in mind, you create a space for it to be realized in your conscious life experience. You might be surprised to discover that you actually inhabit a friendly universe. To presume otherwise is, as we have seen, harmful to your health and dangerous to your survival.

Afterword

WE ARE NOW approaching ground zero, the end of the book, and reentry into the down-to-earth real world. As you prepare to leave, you might like to collect your thoughts and reassemble your belief structure. Perhaps you'd like to repossess your old mind-sets — the lenses you set aside as the price of admission to our magic theatre. Feel free to reclaim them now. I think you'll find them as useful as they ever were.

When you finish the book, look around. If you still see yourself as a spectator or participant in a spectacle from which you separate yourself, perhaps your spectacles need changing. This is especially likely if, in *your* view, your life isn't working. If your life seems satisfactory, and you feel that you're enjoying an adequate share of health and peace of mind, you don't need new lenses, you've got the right idea. If it works, fine! Any action which makes you feel good should be actively continued *as long as it still makes you feel good.*

At this juncture, a brief anecdote will throw my point into sharper focus.

Every day, for twenty-five years, a lady named Blanche

from Brooklyn stepped out onto her front porch in Flat-
bush and shook her feather duster. She faced each of the
cardinal directions, and solemnly shook it three times to
the East, three times to the West, three times to the North
and thrice to the South. On the particular day on which
we observe her, her neighbor Bernie comes out and says,
"Blanche, why are you doing that?"

"To keep the tigers away," she replies, shaking vigorously to the East where Bernie is standing. "But Blanche,"
says Bernie, "there's no tigers in Brooklyn. I lived here for
twenty-five years, and I never seen a single tiger — except
in the zoo."

"Exactly!" beams Blanche as she triumphantly tucks
her clean feather duster under her arm, goes inside, and
triple-locks her door.

Finally, I'd like to leave you with an image — a lens.

The spider,
silently spinning,
weaves her web,
the web of illusion,
then stands at its center
secure in the knowing
that she is the source.

Bibliography

BOOKS

Assagioli, Roberto. *The Act of Will.*New York: Viking Press, 1973.
Benoit, Hubert. *Supreme Doctrine: Psychological Studies in Zen Thought.* New York: Penguin Books, 1968.
Capra, Fritjof. *The Tao of Physics.* Boulder: Shambhala Publications, 1975.
Chafetz, Morris. *How Drinking Can Be Good For You.* New York: Stein & Day, 1978.
Friedman, Meyer and Rosenman, Ray H. *Type A Behavior and Your Heart.* New York: Alfred A. Knopf, 1974.
Harding, M. Esther. *Woman's Mysteries.* New York: Harper & Row, 1976.
Janov, Arthur. *The Primal Scream.* New York: Dell Publishing, 1971.
Jaynes, Julian. *The Origin of Consciousness in the Breakdown of the Bicameral Mind.* Boston: Houghton Mifflin, 1976.
JUNG, CARL G. *On the Nature of the Psyche.* Princeton: Princeton University Press, 1969. *Collected Works, Vol.* 14, "Mysterium Coniunctionis."

Koestenbaum, Peter. *The New Image of the Person.*
Westport, CT: Greenwood Press, 1978.
Kübler-Ross, Elisabeth. *Questions & Answers on Death & Dying.* New York: Macmillan, 1974.
Death: The Final Stage of Growth. New York:
Prentice Hall, 1975.
Kuhn, Thomas S. *The Structure of Scientific Revolutions.*
Chicago: University of Chicago Press, 1970.
Moody, Raymond A. Jr. *Life After Life.* Harrisburg, PA:
Stackpole Books, 1976.
Penfield, Wilder, et al. *The Mystery of the Mind: A Critical Study of Consciousness & the Human Brain.*
Princeton: Princeton University Press, 1975.
Penfield, Wilder & Rasmussen, Theodore. *The Cerebral Cortex of Man: A Clinical Study of Localization of Function.* New York: Macmillan, 1950.
Sagan, Carl. *The Cosmic Connection: An Extraterrestrial Perspective.* New York: Doubleday, 1973.
Selye, Hans. *Stress in Health and Disease.* Ontario:
Butterworth, 1976.
Wilber, Ken. *The Spectrum of Consciousness.* Wheaton,
IL: Theosophical Publishing House, 1977.

ARTICLES

Beecher, H. K. "The Powerful Placebo," *Journal of the American Medical Association,* 24 December 1955.
Cousins, Norman. "The Mysterious Placebo: How Mind Helps Medicine Work," *Saturday Review,* 1 October 1977, pp. 9–16.
Cerottini, J. C. "Lymphoid Cells as Effectors of Immunologic Cytolysis," *Hospital Practice,* no. 12, November 1977, pp. 57–68.

Darby, William J. "The Benefits of Drink," *Human Nature,* November 1978, pp. 30–37.

Jones, Tony, ed. "In Memory's Eye," *Quest,* November–December 1977, pp. 113–128.

Krahenbuhl, J. L. & Remington, J. S. "Immunotherapy and Cancer," *Human Nature,* January 1978, pp. 78 & ff.

Yano, K.; Rhoads, G. G.; and Kagan, A. "Coffee, Alcohol and Risk of Coronary Heart Disease among Japanese Men Living in Hawaii," *New England Journal of Medicine,* Vol. 297, pp. 405–509.

LAST LETTER TO THE PEBBLE PEOPLE
By Virginia Hine
"All who love must one day die. All lovers must, at some time, be stretched in grief across the ultimate chasm for which the little deaths that punctuate the course of deep love have only imperfectly prepared them. Only by experiencing this stretching have I come to know that bereavement is a necessary stage in the growth of love. As life fulfills itself in love, so love, fulfills itself in death. To record the process through which one family came to know this truth in the deepest places of their souls is the final purpose of this book." From the Foreword.

"To say that I enjoyed it immensely is somehow not quite right unless you will read enjoyment as the equivalent of very meaningful. It is a book about love and the human connection . . . the building of bonds stripped of artifice and social amenities."

— Eric Cassell, M.D.
Cornell University Medical College

"I just finished reading Last Letter and am profoundly touched. I feel it is one of the most important and beautiful statements on death ever."

— Jeanne Achterberg, Research Scientist

$5.95 Quality Paperback